The author

Ian Ruskin-Brown MSc. MIMgt. MCIM. DipM. FInstSMM. MMRS.

Ian, formerly an academic, is now a practising and incurable author, businessman and trainer. Over the last 30 years he has gained a wide range and depth of experience in marketing and in management. He is a full member of the Chartered Institute of Marketing, the Business Graduates Association of MBAs, a fellow of the Institute of Sales and Marketing Management, a full member and qualified as a Diplomate of the Market Research Society, and a member of the British Institute of Management.

Ian's business career has a strong bias toward marketing management, in the operational field and planning functions – including working for companies such as J Lyons and Co., Reed Paper Group, Trebor Sharpes, Esso Petroleum and Goodyear Tyre and Rubber.

Following a major motor accident in 1973, his career had oriented toward the academic, and consultancy, working as a Senior Lecturer at the SWRMC (now the University of the South West) and with visiting lectureships at the Universities of Bath, Bristol, Oran (Algeria) and the NIHE Limerick (Eire).

For 13 years Ian was a member of the Faculty of the Chartered Institute of Marketing (CIM), and was recently made a member of the IBM International Business School. For these and other bodies, he has run open and client-specific courses at home and abroad.

Ian has specialised in the service industries and has carried out much in-house work, on a national and international basis, for a wide range of companies.

Before taking up founding Directorships in several very successful companies, MSS Market Research Ltd and Mercator Ltd (MR Software), Ian worked as an independent, freelance consultant, being involved in consumer, industrial, Government policy and tourism projects, often acting in the dual capacity of consultant/project leader.

In early 1983, Ian set up his own independent marketing consultancy, now operating as Ruskin Brown Associates, for training in marketing and sales skills and for the provision of both consultancy and market research services. This activity continually brings him into contact with a wide range of marketing situations at home and abroad.

Foreword

This book is designed to be read by practising business people, not academics. It is often said that it is pointless to write for this audience because although they may buy the books, they rarely read them. I believe this behaviour (when it happens) is more a comment on the style of the book, than on the predisposition of business people in general.

I am a market researcher by training and experience, having started and helped to develop three very successful companies in that industry, 'Mercator' (producer of the world's foremost data analysis software for PCs), MSS Market Research, one of the UK's leading full service agencies and Marketing Decisions (now operating as Ruskin Brown Associates) who specialise in helping their clients conduct or buy marketing research more cost effectively.

By vocation I am a trainer and author of training material in marketing topics, over the years having been a member of the faculties of the University of the South West, The Chartered Institute of Marketing, IBM International Business School (and their Marketing University – based in the USA) ICL, CareerTrack International (*with whom I worked with the Tom Peters organisation*), Marcus Bohn Associates and Hawksmere to name just a few.

Too many business books on marketing are either insultingly simplistic, (such as those designed for the sole trader, available via Business Links and the banks) or excruciatingly academic, obtuse, designed to impress other academics, and/or as textbooks for those undergoing some form of Higher Education. This book is different, I hope. As a practical and comprehensive introduction to marketing, it is designed to be read by those in business today. The particular audience in mind being those without any formal marketing training, who are responsible for the defence and development of their company's revenue (or who interface with such people in their company). It will appeal to entrepreneurs with companies employing between 20 and 500 people. As well as those people in larger companies who, through excelling in their technical areas, have been promoted to areas of marketing responsibility, and need to understand the concepts, practices and the language of this (to them perhaps) new and alien discipline.

This book forms the hub of a wheel, the spokes of which examine in more detail the skills and techniques of the individual disciplines that go to make up the craft of marketing. Each one of these 'spokes' will cover one specialism including:

- Marketing strategy and plans
- Marketing a service business
- Marketing communications
- Key account marketing
- Marketing research.

The sequence of the book is designed to take the reader logically through the process of learning about the craft. From why marketing is important to the business, then, via a general overview of how marketing works, to an examination of each of its main pillars:

- choosing the company's markets and customers
- designing the right product
  - at the right price
  - promoting it the right way and
- making it available to the customer in the right place at the right time.

Mastering Marketing concludes with an introduction to the process of understanding what the company is up against in its marketplaces, and the techniques to gather this information.

Wherever pertinent I illustrate much of the content with examples from current real life businesses.

In nearly every chapter there are exercises to enable the reader to consolidate their understanding via application of the chapter contents to their own business situation. I invite readers who may wish to check that they are on the right lines when they address these exercises, to make contact with me via e-mail, attaching their answers to the questions posed. I would also welcome any other feedback, comments, questions or constructive criticism that will help me improve this or subsequent books in the series.

My e-mail address is: ian.ruskin-brown@lineone.net.

In the meantime, I wish you happy reading, and a successful business.

Ian Ruskin-Brown

Contents

Icons

Throughout the Masters in Management series of books you will see references and symbols in the margins. These are designed for ease of use and quick reference directing you quickly to key features of the text. The symbols used are:

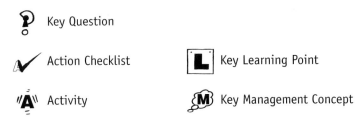

Key Question

Action Checklist   Key Learning Point

Activity   Key Management Concept

We would encourage you to use this book as a workbook, writing notes and comments in the margin as they occur. In this way we hope that you will benefit from the practical guidance and advice which this book provides.

There are exercises throughout this book. For your own convenience, we suggest that you use the sheets provided as a template, reproducing them as required according to the instruction given.

The power of marketing

Effectiveness is more important than efficiency

Chapter 1: Part I

Synopsis

The first part of this chapter examines the major ways in which a company can improve its financial performance, how these ways break down into various strategies and how these strategies are related to the stages of the product life cycle.

It moves on to discuss which of the above strategies have the greatest potency when it comes to making a contribution to financial performance. From this emerges the identification of effectiveness versus efficiency, and then the potency of one versus the other when making contributions to the company's bottom line.

It goes on to establish that revenue generation is an order of magnitude more powerful than cost cutting, i.e. effectiveness is more potent than efficiency. Finally a small exercise is provided to help you assess the effectiveness of your company.

Introduction

There are essentially four ways in which an organisation can improve its financial performance. Neither of these ways are mutually exclusive, any one or combination of the four can be employed at any one time. They are in no particular order of importance:

Action Checklist

- Increasing sales volume

- Increasing price

- Cutting costs

- Reducing investment

Combining price and sales volume produces increased revenue. The last option, reducing investment, assumes that overall revenue and profit are not effected, or at the very least remain static. Although the first three are normally considered to be within the remit of an organisation's management, and the last (reducing investment) the remit of the Board alone, it is interesting to note that although most management have little, if any, direct control over the levels of investment in their own organisation, it is often the case that (particularly in business to business situations) the sales and marketing teams can have an impact on the levels of investment of their customers, via what they sell.

Although these four ways of improving financial performance can be taken in any permutation or combination, the marketer must understand how these impact on the strategy of the company. They must know in what circumstances any particular combination is best employed, and which of these strategies have the most potent impact on the bottom line.

Strategic focus

Key Management Concept

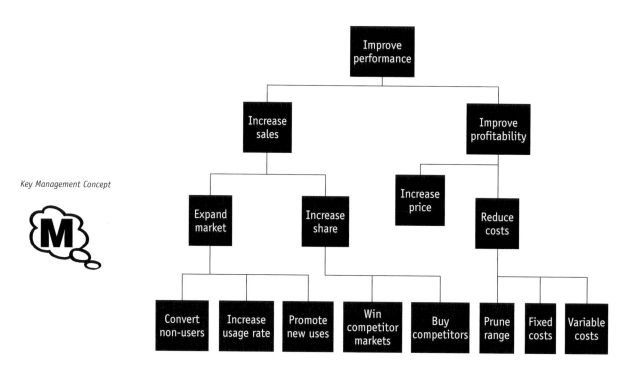

Figure 1.1: An organogram created from the company's three options

Addressing the three options which are within the remit of a company's management we obtain the cascade (or organogram) as shown in Figure 1.1.

We can see from this, that in order to increase sales volume we may need to either expand our marketplace and/or increase our share of that marketplace.

Expanding a market can mean creating new users, or alternatively increasing the rates at which a company's goods or service are used. It could actually include promoting new uses entirely. For example, in the mobile telephone industry, how much of the emphasis during the first few years was to broaden the range of users of mobiles? Firstly, to executive level business people, then management and then into the general population. Within the general population the adult usage was broadened, from adult males, through to adult females and latterly, into teenagers in the family.

Increasing the usage rate of the mobile telephone was initially brought about by lowering the cost of handsets and the subscriptions, and also the cost of the call, and most recently by enabling people to pre-pay for their calls. Examples of new uses for a mobile telephone are as:

- a safety device for a woman alone at night
- a means for parents to stay in touch with children
- a tool for business travellers when abroad, to be able to make contact with the home country.

New uses are constantly being evolved such as links with laptop computers and no doubt the evolution of mobile telephones will continue.

Introducing the product life cycle [PLC]

Key Learning Point

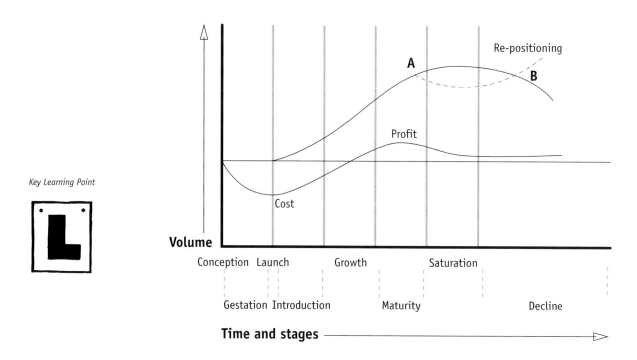

Figure 1.2: A stylised 'PLC'

The product life cycle (PLC) is a very useful framework for thinking about the development of a company's products in its markets. In this context we will briefly examine the basic concept and its stages. After this we will see the implications of the PLC on what business strategies are open to the company for improving the bottom-line in relation to where the product is in its life cycle.

Gestation

This stage is the period between 'conception' and 'launch', during which the 'new product' is being developed and its business future is being planned. At this stage it is all investment so we see that the revenue line is below the horizontal axis. Note, this condition applies well into the next stage (*introduction*) and often into the third stage (*growth*), new products require a lot of support and even then it is no means certain that they will be successful. On average some 15 new ideas have to be launched in an industry before one of them is successful. (*However, take heart, this is an improvement on the attrition suffered some 30 years ago when it took 58 new product ideas to produce one success, and some companies today are much better than the average – especially when they do their market research – see Chapter 7.*)

Introduction

At this stage the company is concerned to get customers to buy the product for the first time as it is by no means certain that the product will have a market. Choosing the right customers to target with the marketing support for the 'launch' requires an understanding of:

- What sort of new product it is: is it just a re-vamp (i.e. this *year's* model), a new and/or better way of delivering benefits for which there is an already established market (i.e. a one button, preset number dialling facility on a telephone handset), **or**

- Is it something so radical that it will alter customer's purchase and/or consumption behaviour (e.g. colour printers, e-mail, out-of-town shopping areas, chartered jets for holidays in the guaranteed sun)

and depending on the above…

- Who are the 'innovator' customers and the 'early adopters', and how can the company clearly identify them (*see Segmenting for an IT related market, Chapter 3, page 102*).

Through this, and the next stage, the sales and marketing arms of the company have the potential to seize the initiative in that the customer is immature (in the sense that they are often unsure that the product is for them, how to use it, in what configuration and how to specify it). Thus, the customer is open to as much help as they can get, both in terms of buying and using the product.

Growth

At this stage the potential of the product starts to be exhibited. More and more new customers are drawn to the product and sales volumes start to rise dramatically. Word starts to spread amongst customers and competitors alike. By the latter part of this stage competitors start to realise that this new product is taking some of their business, and if they don't react it could well take more and perhaps all of it. Others, not in the market, are also noticing the success and are forming the intention to enter what is now a proven marketplace so that they can enjoy this new source of profit.

Maturity

Several particular things typify this stage:

- At the beginning of the stage, repeat customers become a significant part of the market, at the end they are the main type of customer in the market.

- Customers are getting 'mature' in that they know enough about the product to start specifying exactly what they want – indeed, they start behaving like 'buyers' (who have the initiative because they are no longer dependent on help from the sales and marketing arms of the vendor).

- The rate of entry of new competitors to the market reaches its peak, and so does the intensity of competition. The consequence of this is that there is a downward pressure on margins. Even if there is no price war – which frequently does break-out – the pressure of having to compete will force extra expenditure to be made on promotion of one sort or another, all of which carries a cost.

- Discerning people in this market can, if they bother to look, often espy the seeds of what will eventually supplant the product e.g. the railways and Henry Ford and/or the Wright Brothers; IBM and Apple etc. This is the point in time (point 'A' in Figure 1.2, page 12) at which plans for repositioning the product should start to be laid. It is dangerous, particularly nowadays (as IBM found), to ignore these thunder clouds on the horizon, or to wait until they start to have an effect on the business (point 'B' in Figure 1.2, page 12) before taking action. The chief reason IBM was able to survive was its size and the depth of its purse.

Saturation

Nearly every customer here is a *repeat* customer. The main source of new customers is maturation i.e. those that move into the market by virtue of where they are on some family or business life cycle (e.g. prams and pushchairs are acquired for mothers or mothers to be, usually not before; computer servers and intranet systems are acquired by companies that have reached a certain size, before this they offer few benefits worth the cost etc.). During 'saturation' competition is at its most intense, there is only one way to grow for any player in this market, and that is to take business from the competition, to take the food from their plate (so to speak), which they notice, resent and can be expected to react against.

Decline

A product's life cycle decline is caused by its market disappearing. This may happen in a number of ways, because the customer's needs:

- no longer apply (e.g. tin baths, and 'buggy whips': people have hot water systems and few drive horse drawn buggies etc.) or

- are now being satisfied via a product that, in some way, is more attractive to the customers (e.g. with the exception of Holland, cars have largely replaced bicycles as a means of getting to and from work in western Europe. A car keeps you dry when it rains, warm when its cold, and is less tiring. Thus it allows you to reach a place of work many more miles from where you live, or to live many miles from where you have to work).

Strategic focus and the product life cycle

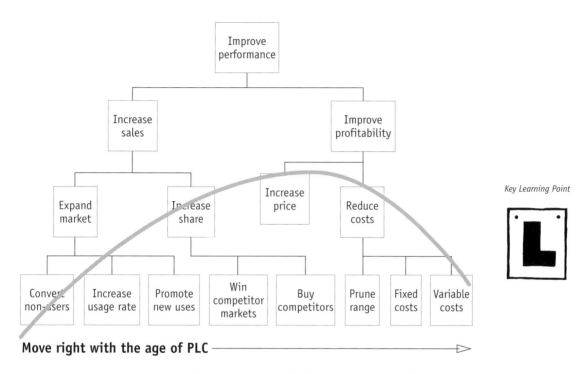

Key Learning Point

Figure 1.3: Strategic focus – managing the product/s

Taking the organogram in Figure 1.1, but now with the product life cycle super-imposed as in Figure 1.3, we can see that 'expanding the market' is suitable emphasis for the early stages of a product life cycle. During the following growth and maturity phases, (where competition starts to get quite intense), the business emphasis moves towards defending and/or increasing one's market share. This can be obtained by either beating the competitor in the marketplace e.g. the launch of 'Orange' in the British market, or, if that's too expensive, then it might be worth considering buying the competition. This last option is perhaps more suitable for the saturation stage of the life cycle when there might be companies available for sale because they are more geared up to exploit growth, than to manage themselves in a steady state market, and are thus vulnerable.

At the saturation and decline stage the emphasis of the company must be to reduce costs to the absolute minimum. The market is not going to go anywhere and the emphasis therefore is to milk as much profit as can be obtained from static and eventually declining sales. In simple terms as shown on Figure 1.3, the cost reduction exercises normally fall into four basic areas – the reduction of:

- inventory carrying costs
- production costs which accompany the reduction in the size of the range
- fixed costs and
- variable costs.

Excessive attention is frequently paid to the reduction of fixed costs. In many cases that means reducing the size of the workforce, which is perhaps the largest single fixed cost a company may have. It may also involve getting rid of production facilities and deciding to 'out-source' during this particular stage of the life cycle. Out-sourcing is a very potent way, if employed wisely, of making dramatic reductions in the cost of facilities. It is also interesting to note that out-sourcing can also have the effect of reducing the amount of capital employed, i.e. the fourth area of improving financial performance as mentioned above.

Lastly the reduction of variable costs should be addressed, assiduously. Actions to do this will range from:

- re-engineering the product, (so that it can be produced more cheaply), and/or bringing great pressure to bear on suppliers, (so that they reduce their prices to the company) to
- rationalising the company's logistics so that the costs of transportation are reduced to the minimum.

Relative potency

The strategies outlined in Figures 1.1 and 1.2, are often more appropriate in one set of circumstances in relation to the product life cycle than other periods. In addition to this they have different levels of power to make a contribution to the bottom line of the company. We illustrate this in Figure 1.4 below.

	A	B Effect of 1% improvement on labour costs	C	D Effect of 1% improvement all round	E	F
Discount	Nil	Nil	Nil	Nil	Nil	
Price/hour	£25	£25		@£25.25		*Improvement*
Volume +/–	4hrs	4hrs	4.04hrs			
Revenue [£]	100	100			102.01	£2.01
Cost of sales* *£7.50 labour £7.50 materials	60	59.7	4.04hrs	@£14.85	59.994	60.6p
Gross profit	40	40.3			42.016	
Overheads per day	30	30	99%		29.7	30p
Net profit	10	10.3			12.316	
% profit +/–	–	+3%			+23.16%	

Key Learning Point

Figure 1.4: Relative potency

In Figure 1.4, we've taken a hypothetical circumstance of a company in the service sector selling its service by the hour. For example, a small word processing or desk top publishing bureau. In column A a rather simple profit and loss situation is outlined. Following it through:

- the company is charging its service at £25.00 per hour
- it is being offered business to the tune of four hours work

therefore potentially generating a revenue of £100.00.

The cost of sales is made up of £7.50 per hour of labour and £7.50 per hour of consumable materials, (such as, toner, paper, electricity) i.e. £15 per hour. Thus for all of four hours, the variable costs come to £60 which gives a gross profit of £40.00 to the company.

Say the company had approached its overhead attribution on a daily basis and that its gross overhead, rent, rates, fixed labour costs came to some £6,000.00 a year. If there are 200 working days in any one year, that equates to £30.00 per day. So, deducting this from gross profit we see that, in column A everything else being equal, an order for four hours worth of work will produce a net profit (if no other business is done that day) of £10.00 for the day.

In column B we demonstrate the effect of applying the strategies outlined to the right of the organogram shown in Figures 1.1 and 1.3. What we are doing is reducing costs by, for example, reducing the cost of labour. If we reduce the cost of labour by 1% this will have the effect of reducing the cost of sales by 30p in total. Thus, if we don't erode that saving, we put 30p directly on the bottom line, making the net profit £10.30. In other words, for a reduction of 1% on labour, we have improved net profitability by 3%. Quite a potent trick and one that is the pride of the accountancy profession. It certainly tends to impress other people in the organisation who are often mystified by the way that a 1% reduction in cost can multiply to a 3% increase in net profit.

However, this magic has its limitations. Firstly, there is a limit to the extent by which management can cut the costs of a company before damaging the ability of that company to compete in the marketplace, (certainly in the long-term and frequently in the short-term as well). Secondly, this approach tends to blind people in the organisation to the potency of increasing sales (they see reduced costs as a certainty but increasing sales as only a probability).

Columns C, D, E and F in Figure 1.4 illustrate the Kaizen approach to improving the bottom line. In other words, making a 1% improvement to every single part of the business that we can. Thus we see that:

- the volume has been increased by 1% (or 2.4 minutes)

- the price has been increased by 1% which means to say that it is now being charged out at £25.25 per hour.

The effect of these two factors is to produce an increase in revenue to £102.01, (i.e. an increase of £2.01).

Continuing the improvement

We reduce the cost of sales, both labour and materials by 1%, (this means to say that each hour is now costing us only £14.85). For the total deal therefore the cost is £59.99 giving us a gross profit of £42.01. Reducing our overheads by 1% as well, in other words 30p, (remember this does not go up pro rata with volume, it is a truly fixed cost) this provides us with a net profit of £12.31, which is an increase of 23.16% over our basic profit in column A.

It is important to note that of the total 23.16%, 20.1 percentage points have been derived from an increase in sales revenue (volume and value) and only 3.16 percentage points have been derived from a reduction in costs. In other words, the left hand sides of Figures 1.1 and 1.3 are more potent in terms of their ability to contribute to the bottom line than the right hand strategies. Thus, for a fairly simple profit and loss account, with the ratios as shown in column A, the left hand side's strategies of Figure 1.3 are seven times more potent than are the right. This is the difference between effectiveness and efficiency.

The effectiveness efficiency grid

In Figure 1.5 below, the effectiveness efficiency grid is shown as a 2 x 2 matrix. Effectiveness is doing the right thing, addressing those issues that are important to the success of the organisation. This would be, for example, obtaining the best possible price which means selling to the most lucrative customers and also perhaps the customers with the greatest ability to buy volume, the highest usage rates and so forth. Efficiency is all about keeping costs down, getting more bang for the buck; reducing wastage. In other words, efficiency is about doing things well or as we say in the diagram, doing things right.

Key Management Concept

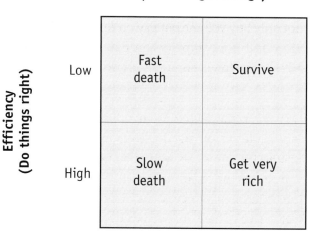

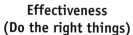

Figure 1.5: *Effectiveness – efficiency grid*

We can see from Figure 1.5 that an organisation which is not doing the right things is low in effectiveness, and if it's not doing it right it's low in efficiency as well. This will predicate a fairly quick demise for such an organisation. An example could be that the company is producing a first class product but is trying to sell it to the wrong customers, at the wrong price, and it is fairly poor at controlling its costs. In all but the most exceptional circumstances, such as if the company were a monopoly, (see Part II) that company would die fairly quickly.

The reflex of the financial controllers of most companies is often to ensure that costs are kept to the minimum, in other words, efficiency is a matter of priority. However, we see in the bottom left quadrant of this matrix that this approach, if taken alone, predicates a slow death. The company still hasn't got the right customers who are capable of buying the right volumes at the best possible prices, and the subsequent death will be slow and painful, but inevitable none the less. The top right of the matrix suggests that it is possible for an inefficient company to survive – indeed there is much evidence that goes further and says that an unprofitable company can survive, in the short-term at least. Good customers not only buy volume but pay on time, which confers the benefit of positive cash flow and if a company can pay its bills it will not be made bankrupt, i.e. it will survive (maintaining positive cash flow is an effectiveness strategy).

Of course, the ideal is for a company to be high in effectiveness, in other words going for the best possible customers, those prepared to pay the highest price and consume the largest volumes, as well as being very efficient about doing this. In these circumstances the organisation will become very rich indeed. Any approach to business that helps to generate and/or to increase sales revenue for a company, is 'effective'. There are two basic approaches to business which are 'effective' by nature, they are:

- a sales philosophy and
- a marketing philosophy.

A sales philosophy focuses on the skills of persuading customers to buy from one's own company rather than from the competition. As opposed to a marketing approach which is a business philosophy that focuses on finding out what it is the customer wants, is willing to pay for and that the company can produce at a profit.

The company then produces 'products' that satisfy those wants and makes them available for purchase.

In reality of course, sales and marketing are but two sides of the same coin. As an old sales proverb has it, 'no company ever sold a bad product twice'. As most marketers would recognise 'nothing actually happens until somebody sells something'.

Key factors for marketing effectiveness

1. Environmental sensitivity
Sound research/analysis of how the market is changing, leading to a more proactive approach. Quick feedback mechanisms on success/failure.

Key Management Concept

2. Tight customer focus
Knowing who your chosen customers are, where they are and what they want. Targeting of the offering and all marketing activities rather than a 'catch-all' approach.

3. Balance portfolio

Sufficient products in each of the following categories:

- steady revenue earners

- growth products and

- products for the future.

These should all be managed appropriately to provide a sound business platform. The right balance of marketing and financial objectives will achieve this.

4. Customer orientation

Customers believe the company is 'good to do business with'. This is essential for loyalty and as a platform for future acceptability. This has to be a 'top-down' commitment with no deviations.

5. Commitment to innovation and improvement

Not only in design, quality and performance but in new and better ways of handling the business.

6. Recognition of need for organisational adaptation

Flexible, alert, prepared to change 'old ways'. Helped by 'flat' structures, shared objectives and effective teamwork.

7. Understanding competitive advantage

Commitment to being 'better than competition' in ways to which customers will respond positively. Not being 'equal' or just using reactive 'bench marking' to mimic others, but 'setting the agenda' for others to follow.

8. Clear, realistic product line strategic objectives

Helped by good portfolio thinking. Not trying to maximise profit, share or growth inappropriately or 'equally', on all products in all markets. Avoiding 'macho' targets which will require 'market forcing' and lead to problems in the long-term. Understanding the need for product 'image' as well as performance objectives.

9. 'Tight-loose' control systems

Understanding what needs to be tightly controlled or standardised, and what needs adaptation to market, or local input and accountability, to be fully successful.

10.Long-term orientation

Not looking only for short-term profit, but investing in image and a strong long-term market position as a foundation for future profit.

(The above list is adapted from IBM Marketing University Module 'B' 1998)

However, as attractive as the left hand sides of the strategy shown in the Figures 1.1 and 1.3 (page 10, 17) may appear to be, it is not always possible to adopt them. Market conditions may well predicate the right hand strategies (*efficiency*) are more appropriate at the time. The market conditions which may inhibit or permit a company's freedom of manoeuvre are very much tied in with the law of supply and demand which is the topic we address next.

But, before you proceed – have a go at assessing how '**effective**' your company is.

Activity No. 1

Your effectiveness

The ten factors listed below are most commonly given as a key to effectiveness.

A. Rank them in their relative importance for achieving improved effectiveness for your company today and next year. **10 = high, 1 = low.**

B. Then for each factor in turn, rate your present effectiveness on a scale of 1-10. **1 = low, 10 = high.**

C. Multiply 'A' by 'B' for each factor. Add up all these products.

D. What conclusions emerge?

Factor	A How do you rank these in your company?	B Your company's rating 1-10	A x B
1. Environmental sensitivity			
2. Tight customer focus			
3. Balanced portfolio			
4. Customer orientation in all functions			
5. Commitment to innovation and improvement			
6. Recognition of need for organisational adaptation			
7. Understanding of competitive advantage			
8. Clear product line strategic objectives			
9. Tight/loose control system			
10. Long-term orientation			
		Total	

Conclusions

Consider: Maximum score is 550.

If your rankings are right then the scores equal:

550-500	You are doing very well, unless you are fooling yourself
499-450	Fair, but could try harder/smarter
449-400	This book is essential for you
<400	You have some major changes to make to your corporate culture. Do that **before** you apply this book.

The power of marketing

The law of supply and demand

Chapter 1: Part II

Synopsis

Part II sets out to examine how the law of supply and demand will determine which of the three main business orientations an organisation must adopt in order to succeed. In conjunction with the first part of this chapter it will establish why a marketing orientation is essential for the successful running of most businesses today.

Introduction

As a method of generating sales revenue, however, marketing is not the be-all and end-all of running a business. There are at least two other business philosophies which are capable of producing lots of revenue profitably under the right circumstances. Indeed, marketing can be said to be the least favoured option in that as a business concept it is the most difficult to put into practice, it requires special and scarce talent. It is also the most expensive way to operate. If a company does not have to adopt a marketing stance, then the 'best advice' is that it should not bother. The problem is, however, that the circumstances under which any alternative to marketing can be adopted, are getting fewer and further between. What are these alternatives, and under what circumstances would they prove more profitable than marketing? To address that question we have to start at the very basic link in the chain of business, the process from which profit is derived.

The basic link in the chain

Like all good ideas, the way that profit is derived is quite a simple concept, it is the practice that can prove hellishly difficult. The principle is to buy well, and to sell well, such that the total costs incurred by the company are more than covered by the income derived from what the company sells. When income is greater than expenditure, the company is profitable, when income does not cover expenditure the company is making a loss and under all normal circumstances it will eventually fail.

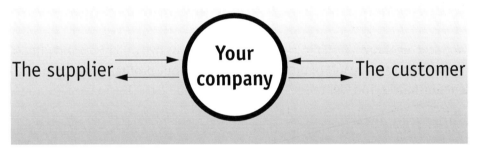

Figure 1.6: The essential dynamic

The essential dynamic therefore as shown in Figure 1.6 is but one link in a chain which stretches from the raw material producer to the eventual consumer. At this point it is worth taking short diversions down two tributaries:

- In business to business situations, i.e. where the customer is another company, it is the consumer markets at the end of the chain that initiate the demand from which the company will derive its income eventually (*there is only one exception to this rule that we know of, the defence industry*).

- At both interfaces between the company and its suppliers, and between the company and its customer, there is a struggle as each party tries to get the best possible deal for themselves.

The company is in turn, both a customer of its suppliers, and a supplier of its customers. (*To leap ahead for a moment, even before we have defined what marketing is, it can be seen from this that the customer can in no way be regarded as a passive element in this process. Therefore, the conventional view of marketing, 'what sellers do to buyers,' can be very misleading. The more useful view is that marketing is what sellers **and** buyers do between themselves.*)

Hard/sellers markets

If the business situation is as portrayed by Figure 1.6, there is not really a market. For a market to exist there has to be alternative suppliers and alternative customers.

This Figure.1.6 situation is therefore a monopoly. The supplier and the company are 'the only game in town', the customer has no other source of supply and must pay the price demanded, or go without.

Where a few suppliers exist and there are lots of customers, the situation is hardly any better, this we call an oligopoly. An example of these types of business situations are to be found in the UK and EU telecomms industries. BT and Mercury being the main carriers in the UK and each other EU country having mainly the state monopoly. (*Throughout the world this is changing as more and more governments open up their mobile/wireless telephony to more and more competition, via the issuing of licences to companies other than their indigenous state telecomms*). Another example is the UK utilities industries where the ordinary person must take their water, gas or electrical power from the one pertinent local supplier available.

'Hard markets' provide a vendor with the greatest freedom to manoeuvre. However, the monopoly [or ologopolistic] company in the 'market' will most often pursue profit maximisation via the adoption of one (or a combination) of two available strategies, which in no particular order are:

- screwing down costs as far as possible, and
- 'jacking-up' prices as much as possible. (i.e. an efficiency strategy re. Figure.1.3).

Freedom to manoeuvre in the first stratagem may be constrained by legislative imperatives, possibly including quality specifications.

On the second issue monopolies/oligopolies will restrict their capacity so that 'supply' is always less than underlying demand. That way, price can be used as a tool to manage real demand (*i.e. a 'want' with the money to pay for it*). Price is raised to the point where demand falls off to meet the capacity available. There is no sense for a monopolist to invest in new plant and equipment so as to increase capacity. Such investment only makes sense if it leads to substantial reductions in the cost of production.

The key question for a business to address in a 'hard market' is:

How does the business produce more, efficiently?

Key Question

This approach to running the business is alternatively referred to as:

- **Production orientation** if producing goods, or
- **Operations orientation** if providing a service.

These companies have little if any intrinsic need for marketing, they have no competitors, and if the customer does not like what they are offering at the price demanded, there will be plenty more customers who may not be so inhibited.

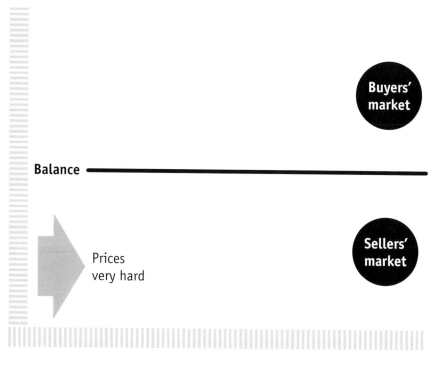

Monopoly/oligopoly pricing = supernormal profits

Figure 1.7: Law of supply and demand

Figure. 1.7 shows this situation. Below the horizontal central axis, markets are under supplied, they are therefore sellers markets and there is no pressure at all on prices. Such companies are said to operate in 'hard markets', that is to say prices are hardened, because customers can do very little by way of getting a price concession.

What small amount of marketing may be exercised by oligopolies or monopolies is usually aimed at increasing traffic, particularly at slack times so as to increase the utilisation of capacity.

An example of this would be BT promoting very cheap (*late evening or very early morning*) calls to friends and relations in Australia. The call traffic so generated will use exchange capacity that would otherwise be lying idle at that time of day in the UK.

Occasionally some oligopoly/monopoly companies may adopt a marketing orientation, but this is usually because they are subject to indirect competition, i.e. prospects customers are experiencing competitive demands on their limited resources of time and/or money. What the prospect spends on his/her mortgage, they are unable to spend on new gas appliances etc.

N.B.   A 'PROSPECT' is a known member of the population toward whom the 'company' is targeting its sales efforts, but has yet not purchased.

As they are operating in hard and sellers markets, such companies will be inherently more profitable than those that are not so privileged.

Most oligopoly/monopoly situations are re-enforced by, if not actually established, in law. Such things as the old General Post Office monopoly for the distribution of letters, or the operation of the telephone system, or the Pilkington's Patent on the float glass method for producing window glass are just two from many examples. This legislation keeps competitors out of the 'frame', but when it is removed they swarm in like bees to the honey pot, to share in the greater than normal profitability.

Supply = demand, therefore sales orientation

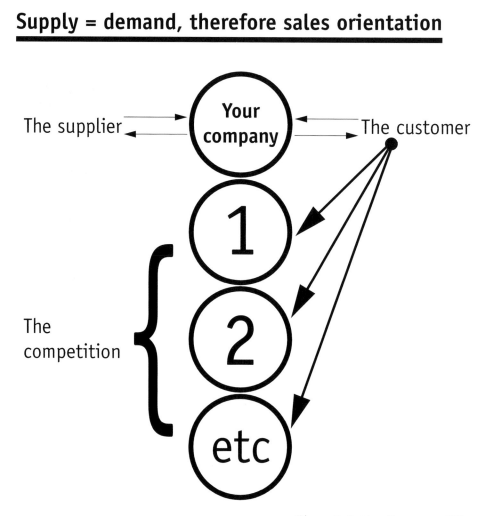

The supplier

Your company

The customer

The competition

1

2

etc

Figure 1.8: Creating competition

Figures 1.8 above, and 1.9 opposite show the situation. New companies entering the market increase supply. Prospects and customers can now canvas alternative suppliers, the effect is thus to create competition. Eventually this competition starts to soften prices.

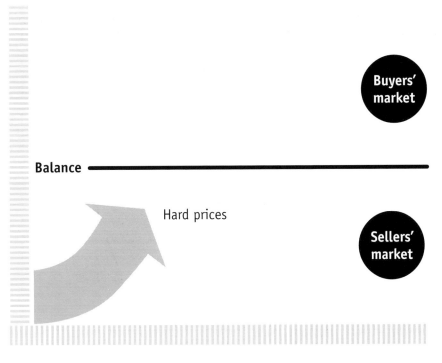

Competitors attracted to the market by these supernormal prices

Figure 1.9: Law of supply and demand

Whilst supply and demand are in a reasonable balance, however, there are alternatives to competing on price, the most popular of which is for the company to 'promote' its wares more effectively than the competition.

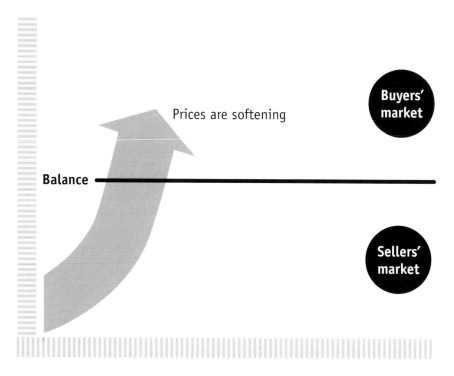

Prices are softening

Balance

Buyers' market

Sellers' market

Competitors enter the market – capacity rises to meet demand

Figure 1.10: Law of supply and demand

The key question for a business to address when there is a balance between supply and demand is:

Key Question

How do we persuade prospects to purchase from us rather than our competitors?

The main aim for such promotion at this stage in the game is to persuade the prospect or customer to buy from the promoter in preference to anyone else. When this is the case we refer to the company as being 'sales oriented'.

Advertising is a child of sales orientation, it is not marketing per se though it is one of the tools of marketing as we will see. Advertising is only one of the many and varied elements of the promotional mix available to business. The job of promotion is to 'move the customer along the buying process' toward the promoter, rather than the competition. In simple terms, promotion accomplishes its task via making a sales proposition to the prospect.

The Lever proposition last century, that 'Cleanliness is next to Godliness', persuaded the working class chapel goers of the North West to wash a little more often, especially on Sundays, and as a result a tremendous amount of Sunlight soap was sold. However, anyone could have claimed as much, and indeed the sales of soap so stimulated were not confined to 'Sunlight', but increased the whole market.

Oversupply brings the danger
of commodity trading

As is illustrated in Figure.1.10, because markets are essentially an expression of human behaviour, like the various 'Gold Rush' episodes of the last century, the numbers of people (*and through them businesses*) drawn to a given commercial opportunity are not at first limited to the purchasing capacity of the market. Almost always more supply enters the newly identified opportunity than the market can bear, with the result that very soon the market is oversupplied with a vengeance and customers are spoilt for choice.

This excess of choice allows the customer to become an active arbiter within the marketplace. The customer shops around and directly or indirectly plays one supplier off against another.

At this point suppliers will need to compete in order to survive, and the natural tendency is for severe price competition to take place as more and more suppliers chase fewer and fewer buyers. Unless suppliers take a company hold on the situation, price will become the focus of competition because the buyers are out for a better deal, and they will tend to try to simplify the task of buying so as to obtain:

- **the best price for:**
  - **a given** (common?) **specification**, and
  - **a given** (common?) **availability**.

Specification and availability are made common in order for the buyer to be able to compare like with like.

In a buyers' market, prices are said to be soft because the buyer drives down the price with little if any regard for the suppliers' welfare.

Key Management Concept

These conditions are known as COMMODITY TRADING. Unless companies adopt deliberate positive strategies to counteract these natural forces, all markets will tend toward this direction.

The consequences of this are shown in Figures 1.11 and 1.12.

Key Learning Point

The weakest companies will collapse as downward pressure on prices erodes profit margins, capacity will be reduced, and as capacity falls dramatically below demand – **it becomes a sellers' market once more.**

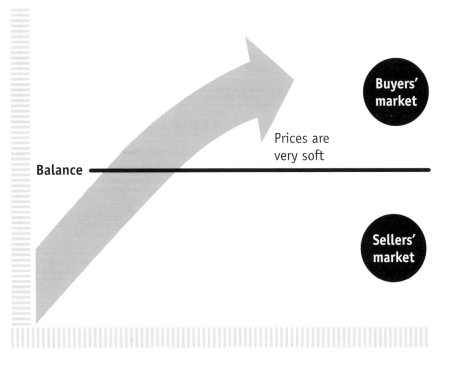

The market is saturated and buyers are spoilt for choice

Figure 1.11: Law of supply and demand

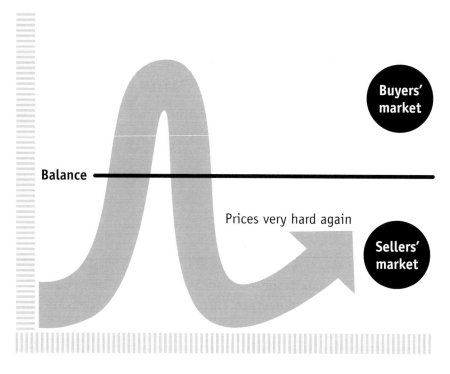

**The market restructures as firms collapse or
are taken over and supply dwindles**

Figure 1.12: Law of supply and demand

This is one of the basic business cycles, it is as old as commerce, and was noted by Adam Smith in his *Wealth of Nations*. The periodicity of the cycle depends upon the individual characteristics of the industry in question.

Surviving oversupply

There are basically only two ways to survive 'commodity trading' so as to be one of the few companies that enjoy the fruits of the hard markets to come.

The first, and most favoured is 'agglomeration', this is because traditionally it has been the most easy to adopt and to apply. Agglomeration is where companies come together, usually by acquisition, so that existing fat and/or muscle is used to obtain more fat and muscle, this is to ensure that companies end up with more power and endurance than the competition.

This process creates so called conglomerates. Some of the world's major commercial empires are thus formed. The most successful of these empires, like the Hanson Trust, are those which have adopted strategies to spread risk and areas of interest. These behemoths spread their range of acquired businesses across a number of counter-cyclical markets. This is to ensure that companies in the group that are going through the rough time of 'soft markets', can be supported by those in the group, which at that time, are enjoying the better profitability of 'hard markets'.

The second stratagem, and the only one open to the smaller company when entering 'soft markets', is to focus the business on the needs of the customer, by asking the third type of seminal question:

What do our (potential) customers want, and are willing to pay for at a price, that allows us to supply at a profit?

This is commonly known as a MARKETING ORIENTATION.

Key Question

The marketing concept introduced

Thus, instead of the business offering the market what it wants to produce, it produces what the customer wants to buy! An apparently simple concept, that like most good ideas is often more easy to preach than to practice. The key issue at the heart of a 'marketing orientation' is what can be called the 'competitive edge', in other words, what makes the company's offering so different from that of the opposition? A sales orientation makes propositions to the market based on the company's perspective. Whereas the marketer will base the proposition on a competitive edge that is valuable to the customer. *(Formally known as the 'Competitive Differential Advantage' – CDA.)*

To illustrate via the use of a consumer good, – say, frozen peas:

> The 'sales-oriented' company would make propositions that their peas were bigger (*or smaller*), greener, fresher, withstood freezing longer, etc. than the competition. They may even go on to offer special deals such as 'This week's special offer, *buy two and get one free*, *collect the packets to get a special premium 'gift'*, *free delivery* (if business to business) etc. The list can be as long and as ingenious as the mind is fertile.

The 'marketing oriented' company will first ask the prospective customer (prospect), what they wished to use the peas for, and then base their product and offering on satisfying the needs thus revealed.

So that for business to business:

- The restaurateur will be offered petit-pois to delight the most jaded pallet (*because he/she is buying customer satisfaction for their restaurant, not peas*).

- The hospital dietitian will be offered peas that meet the nutritional requirements of the nursing regime.

- The local education authority will be offered peas for school dinners that:
  - will retain texture for up to three hours to allow for central cooking and subsequent distribution, and when the kids get to them – are guaranteed bullet proof.

And for consumers:

- The mothers of families will be offered:

  - economy packs for the freezer,

  - peas mixed with diced carrots for attractive meals,

  - sugar-snaps for that intimate 'tête-à-tête' meal with hubby, after a long week, when the kids are in bed.

- Those on their own, such as pensioners, and the like will be offered:

  - single portion packs,

  - perhaps products suitable for the microwave.

This approach, tailoring the competitive edge to the needs of the prospect, is primarily aimed at defending price by creating a differential which is not only attractive to the customer, but also inhibits the potential customer's ability to compare like with like when shopping around. It really works well, when the prospect believes that the value of the perceived differential is worth any extra price [or whatever else they may have to forego] in order to acquire the offering.

The critical issue for a marketing orientation is:

Key Management Concept

> **To know what the prospect/customer wants, and what price they are willing to pay for it.**

Action Checklist

However, not only is this difficult in itself, but in addition, the three questions below are **NOT** mutually exclusive for the marketer:

- How do we produce/operate more efficiently?

- How do we persuade people to buy from us?

- What do people want, that they are willing to pay for?

In order to be successful, the marketer will see these central questions as being critically interdependent, in that:

- no matter how good the competitive differential, if customers are not made aware of:

  – its existence,

  – how and where it can be obtained, and

  – for how much money, (*raising this awareness being in the realm of sales activity*)

  They will not be able to buy, and no matter how good the sales, if the costs of production/operation are not under control, the company can, and often will, bleed to death.

So far this argument has established that, for optimum business results, a company should adopt the business orientation appropriate for the stage of the supply and demand cycle applying to its market at that time.

If supply and demand were the only consideration, companies without the muscle necessary to dominate their market, should be flexible enough to stay in step with, though perhaps slightly ahead of, their market's supply and demand cycle. However, as we shall see in Chapter 6 there are forces in addition to 'supply and demand' that ensure that nowadays, most companies have little option other than to adopt a marketing orientation if they wish to do more than just 'scrape by'.

How marketing works

Chapter 2

Synopsis

'Marketing is a dialogue over time with a specific group of customers/prospects whose needs you get to know in depth and for whom you develop a specific offering with a (*sustainable*) differential advantage over that of your competitors.

'*When you have that advantage, you shout it from the rooftops, if you don't have it you keep quiet until you do!'*

Prof. Malcolm MacDonald, Cranfield

Introduction

The quote above is one of the most useful definitions of the marketing process that has ever been written. It will be the theme for this chapter and its key words and phrases will be used as the section headings. Firstly, a quick analysis of these key phrases:

Key Learning Point

Dialogue over time

Note the word is not 'diatribe', the process must always be two-way. Marketing is a continuous process. The marketer will never completely know the customer, not only do they come to the transaction from different perspectives – one of them is the buyer the other a seller – but customers are dynamic human beings even in business to business situations (*a company never bought anything, it is the people in the company who buy*). Over time people change, as do their needs.

Specific group of customers

First comes the customer, these are the company's most valuable asset, the marketer would do well to calculate the lifetime value of each and every one of the customers the company has. And customers do not come cheap, it costs on average five times as much to gain a customer than to retain them. Almost by definition no marketer can be all things to all people, that way lies commodity trading. The aim therefore is to get as close to these people as possible, and that requires focus on a specific market, and within that market, a specific group of customers, which the marketer calls a 'segment' (see the next chapter). Within this sub-group of customers (i.e. the segment) the marketer must focus on the specific roles that people play when the buying decision is being made.

Key Learning Point

Whose needs are understood in depth

A customer buys to satisfy his/her needs, whatever they may be. The more satisfaction the customer experiences, then the higher the perceived value. This leads to customer loyalty and the lessening of price sensitivity.

Key Learning Point

A specific offer with a differential advantage over that of your competitors

Not only does the company's product have to satisfy the customers' needs, it must do so in a way that is more attractive to the customer compared to what is on offer elsewhere. Because this makes it more difficult for competitors, they will try to outdo the company, to copy if necessary. This means that to stay ahead the marketer must devise some way of sustaining that advantage. The protection available from copyright and patents has its limitations, especially if the competitive differential is 'service'. The only solution is to become a 'learning organisation' and who better to learn from than the customer? This brings us back to the 'dialogue over time'.

Key Learning Point

Specific group of customers

Market selection

Perhaps the most important marketing decision is the selection of the market in which the company is going to do business. Get the right market and the company could flourish, get the wrong market and even with ten times the effort the company could die.

This decision could be taken in one of either two circumstances, either:

'Which new market should the company enter?' – as in the case of an expanding business or starting-up a new business;

Or:

'Is it worthwhile to stay in the company's current market?' In this case the question is, 'Is the business better elsewhere, could there be improved returns for the same efforts in other markets?' i.e. is the grass greener in other markets?

There are several issues which the business must weigh-up in the course of making the market selection decision, they are:

- What is the market worth now?

- What could it be worth in the future?

- Where is the market on its life cycle ?

- How competitive will the company be in the new market? (*i.e. what is the company's potential market share?*)

- What are the barriers to entry, (*old and new markets*)? (*We examine this in more depth in Chapter 3.*)

The customer

It is important to be clear about who the customer is. Companies or countries or any other type of organisation don't buy – they have never bought – it's people who do the buying. People make the decision, use the product, influence and validate other people's purchasing. Therefore for the marketer, understanding about people and what makes them behave the way they do – for both business and consumer markets – is vital.

Understanding of how customers reach buying decisions and what factors influence them is never precise or complete.

It is known that customers are influenced by:

- their needs
- other people
- their personal characteristics
- environment factors, as well as
- the marketing activities of suppliers when forming decisions about:
  - which products to buy
  - from which suppliers
  - how heavily they will use them, etc.

What is not well-understood is exactly what happens in a person's buying decision-making process within the buyer's 'black box' (so to speak).

Clearly, this lack of understanding is important and a marketer must try to gain as much insight as they can for their own situation.

Who buys products?

Customers do not buy products, they buy what products do – for them. Nobody buys a mobile phone. Nobody has ever bought a notebook/laptop. A Mont Blanc pen is not a writing instrument. No company has ever bought a computer! Companies who define their business activities with reference to the industry they are in, or based on the technologies they employ, exhibit a short sightedness which guarantees commercial disaster.

In the case of both the mobile phone and the notebook/laptop at least part of what people buy is communications. Most Mont Blanc pens are bought as gifts, drawing our attention to the important distinction between a *customer* (who pays the bill) and a *consumer* ('the user'). A computer is simply an electronic solution to the age-old problem of information processing (*address lists, accounts, design, calculators etc.*).

The message is that customers purchase items which fulfil their needs and/or solve their problems. They do not buy products. For many years 'products' tended to be narrowly defined around an available technology (*typewriters, mainframes etc.*). Occasionally a brand new solution will emerge (*word processing software, personal computers*) which substantively changes both the need (demand) and the traditional industry structure (supply). For example, Olivetti had to transform itself from a mechanical engineering company, to an electronic engineering company so as to survive in the new era of word processing and electronic communications. How do you define your company, by the technology you use or the solutions your products (*goods or services*) provide to your customers?

The marketer describes a 'product concept' (i.e. the benefits it contains etc.) rather than a 'product'(the feature it contains). In many cases the service support provided with the product is often a far more powerful competitive weapon than the core technologies or features of the product itself. Service (including customer service) is just one example of how the key emphasis should be on product *augmentation* in competitive markets (see Chapter 4, Part I).

Key customer information

It is critical to know the customer's needs, particularly those that are currently unsatisfied.

We also need to understand the criteria used to decide who to buy from. In the PC market, for example, such factors often include:

- monitor clarity
- processor speed
- software bundle
- maintenance contracts
- price and terms
- reliability and availability
- the image of the various alternative suppliers.

It is also crucial to understand *who* buys, decides and influences the purchase decision-making unit (DMU). This is discussed separately below.

In addition, it is important to know *when* companies buy. The marketer must research whether this is a continuous and 'flat' process or whether demand cycles, perhaps by the year, season, month, week, day or time of day etc. Investment decisions, particularly for large capital projects, are often strongly influenced by the state of the economy. Firms often buy in the trough so as to be on-line by the peak. This information is very relevant in the context of the marketing mix (see below) especially pricing, promotion and the timing of a product launch.

The marketer must equally understand how customers use their products. Customers often find uses additional to those envisaged by the producer. This knowledge can enable producers to identify and serve new customers e.g. pick-up trucks were developed for commercial customers like builders and farmers but were later sold to the casual outdoor market for consumers as well. Post-it notes were developed for preachers or lawyers to mark papers they needed to refer to quickly when on their feet. Now look at the multitude of uses to which people have put 'post-it notes'.

Understanding how customers vary by the rate they use the product helps to enhance marketing effectiveness and efficiency. Heavy (large volume) users can be given preferential deals to ensure bulk volumes. However, heavy users often have much buying power, and it may be essential to keep a balanced customer portfolio by serving medium or lighter users as well.

A buyer's loyalty also impacts on how the company goes to market. It is easier to retain loyal customers and more expensive to hold those that are fickle. This also has clear implications when trying to sell to a competitor's existing customers. It may be harder to poach your competitor's 'loyals' – but they could be loyal to you too, whereas his 'fickles' could just play one of you off against the other.

Organisational customers versus consumers

Social and cultural factors influence the lifestyles, customs, needs and buying behaviours of consumers. Personal characteristics such as age, gender, education and profession cause differences in buying criteria, as do psychological factors such as attitudes, perceptions and beliefs. Consumer decisions are also affected by the marketing activities of competitors.

Key Learning Point

Even though it's always people who buy, the way organisations buy can differ markedly from consumer buying. Organisational customers are generally fewer, larger and sometimes more geographically concentrated than are consumers. Demand patterns are often substantially more volatile especially in markets for capital goods.

Organisations often recruit specialist sophisticated and trained buying personnel. These customers will make buying decisions focused more on productivity gains, service and financing than do consumers, and they often prefer to buy direct.

Organisational buying decisions are strongly dependent on economic, political, technological and other conditions affecting the attractiveness of the business environment. Similarly, decisions are determined by:

- organisational objectives
- policies and structures
- the characteristics of individuals within the DMU
- internal politics.

Additionally, organisational buying is strongly influenced by the marketing behaviour of suppliers. Of particular value nowadays are the economic benefits arising from the product, services and price offerings, (and other benefits) that materialise when buyers and sellers form strong relationships.

Buy classes

It can often be useful to understand that customer purchases fall into three classes of buying, they are:

- straight re-buys
- new task purchases
- modified re-buys.

Each varies substantially by:

- purchase complexity
- prior buying and usage experience
- perceived buyer risk
- product and supplier research.

Straight re-buys are simply repurchases of a well-tried and trusted item. There is little perceived risk and no research. For example, ink cartridges or toner for the printer or a family's favourite brand of baked beans.

New task purchases are at the opposite extreme. These are usually very complex acquisitions of new items of which the company has little knowledge of the offering or potential suppliers. 'Perceived risk' is therefore very high and pre-purchase research of alternatives by customers is extensive. For example, a family buying its first home or a company installing its first intranet.

Modified re-buys fall anywhere between the two extremes. In the case of a house – it could be the second or third house as the family grows. Or the customer may need to buy a replacement item but something has changed. They may want a faster one, a safer one, a larger one, etc. or perhaps the usual supplier is out of stock or has raised prices. Hence, in both instances, there is some degree of complexity, inexperience, newness, risk and need for research. These factors can all be present, singly or in combination depending on the extent of the alteration in the buying situation.

For marketers the nature of the customer's buy class has a major bearing on marketing priorities.

For straight re-buy customers the onus should be on maintaining high levels of customer satisfaction to deter shopping around. For new task marketers the situation is more complex but involves helping to simplify the buyer's search process, e.g. by offering attractive bundles of benefits and/or customisation. The 'modified re-buy' stage requires the marketer to recognise that the buyer's priorities vary according to where they are between the two extremes of 'new task' and 'straight re-buy'. In all cases, it is essential to understand the purchase class prevailing.

The decision making unit (DMU)

A purchase often involves a number of individuals each in a different role. The main roles are: initiators, specifiers, users, influencers, deciders, buyers, gate-keepers, searchers and validators.

Initiators are the people who begin the purchase process. They are the role-player who first perceives a need that requires a solution. The critical question for the marketer is what triggers the initiation and how can initiators be influenced to get the buying process started.

Users are those who employ or consume the product (*goods or service*). Users often initiate rebuys and are often consulted by other DMU members because they have the most intimate experience of the product. If they are not involved in a change (*e.g. a new word processing programme*) they can, via mis-use, often negate the product benefits required.

Key Learning Point

Influencers are individuals or groups who make inputs to the purchase decision. They may be respected individuals or 'gurus'. They may influence purchases indirectly through media such as books, reports, television programmes and so on. Where influencers are likely to effect several purchases, they can become an important audience with whom marketers must communicate e.g. travel writers help people decide a new holiday destination; or potential IT outsourcing customers hire consultants to help them to reach buying decisions.

Deciders are those with the power and/or financial authority to make the ultimate choice of what to purchase. When a business buys, the decider may be a senior manager for major purchases or a purchasing manager for repeat goods. In a consumer market for example, a family's choice of Disney for a holiday is often decided by the child.

The **buyer** conducts the transaction. In organisational purchases, the buyer receives information from competing suppliers, helps to analyse it and does the paperwork for new task items. In the case of 're-buys' the buyer is often the decider.

Searchers and **gatekeepers** manage the flow of information into the decision-making process, they stand between potential suppliers and others in the DMU. Gatekeepers shut out suppliers from the more influential role players. Searchers actively, but often selectively, introduce potential suppliers to the DMU. One critical supplier task is to identify gatekeepers and searchers so as to obtain access to the DMU.

The individual needs of each member of the DMU, influenced by their own functional roles, are different. Thus, different and separate solutions need to be offered to each of the role players.

For example, in a medium-sized manufacturing company buying an IT system, the DMU is likely to include at least the CEO, the Finance Director, the IT Director, information managers and users, IT maintenance personnel, buyers and probably external consultants. The needs of each could focus on, respectively, returns on investments (ROI), prices and terms, functionality and reliability, simplicity, durability, a quiet life and repeat work. Consumer marketers don't often face this sort of complexity.

The buying decision process

This assumes a rational approach to decision-making although in all types of market the decision is often affected more by emotional motives than rational ones (*i.e. it is people who buy – not organisations*). The process begins with the recognition of a need. This may be that certain stocks are running low (*straight re-buy*) and that replacements are required, or the customer may have encountered a problem for the first time and needs a solution to it (*new task*).

The specification stage is a detailed analysis of the precise requirements and a formal specification of the bundle of benefits required from the product (goods or service).

Supplier research involves identifying the various producers of, and channels involved in, the supply of these products. Supplier selection involves the customer evaluating which vendor will best suit their needs (i.e. they shop around). Many companies conduct comparative vendor analyses in which the capabilities of competing suppliers are contrasted. In both types of markets evaluative criteria will often involve 'support' (*such as training – hotlines etc.*), terms, delivery etc.

The order routine is carried out by the buyer and involves sending in the order issuing a purchase order number and checking its progress until delivery is made.

Following the delivery and use of the product, the purchase is often evaluated against the original requirements. A satisfied customer may place re-buy orders, whereas a dissatisfied one may go elsewhere next time, and can also be the source of damaging word-of-mouth.

Identifying key players in the decision-making unit when dealing with major accounts

Who is involved and what is their role?

People buy from people. This analysis concerns the key people, their attitudes to the purchase and the various suppliers and their inter-relationships. It enables us to plan what we are going to say to each individual involved. The marketer first needs to draw a chart of the people who will exert influence in some way on the buying decision as per the example organisation chart below:

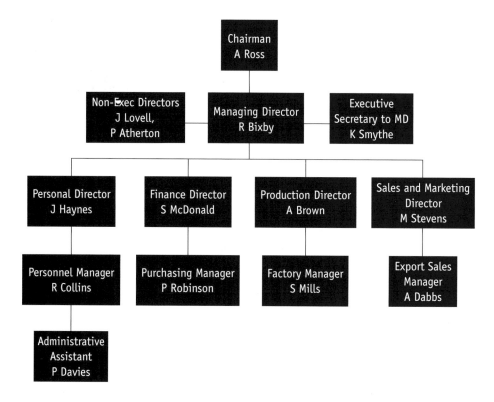

Figure 2.1: Fictional organisational chart

Dialogue over time

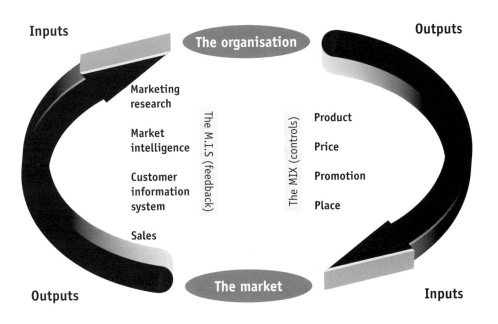

Figure 2.2: The marketing cycle

Figure 2.2 above schematically describes the marketing 'dialogue'. The outbound factors on the right hand side of the diagram are commonly known as the 'marketing mix', which classically contains the four elements of the business within the marketer's control, these are known as the four 'p's which are:

Key Management Concept

- product
- price
- promotion
- place (*standing for 'marketplace', i.e. getting the product to where the customer can buy it*).

This is the 'classic' marketing mix, and we will be examining each element in more detail during Chapter 4.

The classic marketing mix was developed for products which were 'goods', i.e. what was sold was tangible. Nowadays, particularly outside straight re-buy consumer goods, much of what customers buy involves either a pure service (*e.g. package holidays, legal advice buying a house, accountancy, a church wedding etc.*) or a service is used to add value, maybe even the competitive differential (*e.g. delivery, maintenance, training, hotline support, insurance, software etc. for the PC at home or in the office*). Where service is involved in any of these ways, the marketing mix employed must be extended to handle the fact that services are intangible.

This 'extended' mix will additionally include:

- **Physical Evidenc**e (*to 'tangiblise'*).

- **Process** (*to manage the customer's experience*).

- **People** (*service is performed by people, if people are not involved, as is the case of automatic teller machines outside banks, then, it is not a 'service', it is a facility, i.e. incapable of building a favourable relationship between the buyer and the vendor*).

- **Time** (*there are five 'flavours' of time: duration, when available, speed of response, punctuality, and speed of innovation, each of which is capable of providing a competitive advantage*).

- **Resource Management** (*i.e. services are constrained by the capacity of the resources available, e.g. the number of seats on a plane, or free hours in a lawyer's diary, and it is important for the service marketer to manage this capacity so that the company is able to serve customers well at the peak of demand, yet not bleed to death with costly spare capacity during the troughs*).

(*We refer again to this 'extended mix' in Chapter 5, The marketing plan.*)

The conventional view about marketing is to confuse it with the promotion that the business uses to sell its products (*advertising, direct mail, PR, editorial publicity, exhibitions, and the 'message sources' such as: letterhead, cars the sales people drive, the way the call centre deals with customers etc.*). Promotion is certainly the most visible part of the business (*it wouldn't work if it were not visible*), but as can be seen, the whole of this outbound part of the 'dialogue' will be conveying a message to customers, consumers and influencers.

The product must be right, 'you don't sell a bad product twice'. Although this is an old marketing adage it is still very true if a company has to do its business in a competitive marketplace. The price of a product communicates where in the range of things the product is being positioned. To illustrate: the prices of cars indicate where the producer would like us to see them, for example Rolls Royce at the top of the market, Skoda near the bottom end, and BMW, Audi et al, somewhere in the middle. Where the product is for sale also has something to say about where it is positioned, shirts in Harrods would be seen differently from the same shirts available via a mass market mail order catalogue.

But marketing is a 'dialogue' and it is important not to forget that communication is two-way. The business must be asking questions of its customers (*market research*), indeed in an ideal world that is the starting point. Nothing should get made, designed, written, advertised, priced or distributed to the shops until the company knows what it is the customer wants, is willing to pay for at a price that allows the company to do business profitably. Once up-and-running, the dialogue expands to include a listening mode.

For businesses where the buying cycle is fairly short (*e.g. fast moving consumer goods, package holidays, pop concerts etc.*) sales are a quick indicator as to how well the marketing mix is working. Sales can also be made to build database information that will enable the company to see who is buying, what they are buying, when they buy, and perhaps even enable database marketing to be used to target these customers again. Research can be carried out via database strategies to discover which customers are not as responsive as the rest and what can be done about it. Where the marketplace has a long buying cycle (*e.g. new cars, industrial plant and/or equipment, legal advice etc.*) then it will be a while before any given marketing mix will have an effect. In cases such as these, where it can take a long time between the customer or prospect (*i.e. potential customers*) hearing about a product and buying it, the business must monitor how successfully the mix is at moving prospects toward the sale (*see the D.A.G.M.A.R model Figure 4.8, page 182*). This is done via the Customer Information System (CIS) which will comprise an appropriate range of tools (*such as customer satisfaction questionnaires, loyalty measures derived from the database etc.*) to keep the marketer in the picture about how well the marketing mix is working, and to avoid discovering in a couple of years time that it was not right and as a result the customer has purchased elsewhere. (*We cover this in more detail in Chapter 7 'Getting the feedback'*).

Customer's needs, understood in depth

A product is no more than a 'bundle of benefits' which should be tailored to meet the needs of the customer (*see Chapter 4 Part I: The 'product'*). Thus the marketer must know the needs that cause the customer to buy.

A very useful framework for understanding needs is proposed by Abraham Maslow – shown opposite.

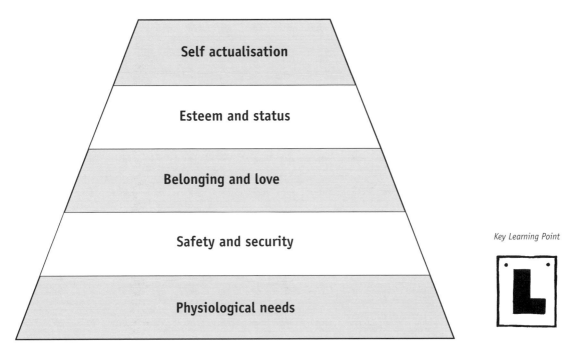

Figure 2.3: Maslow's hierarchy of needs

As a general synopsis: the proposition is that a person's motivation (*in this case to buy*) starts with the most fundamental needs which deal with survival. These are the most potent, and only when they are satisfied (*in order*), can the person start to address the higher order needs. To explain:

'**Physiological needs**' are those which ensure that the person can stay alive, food to eat, water to drink, the right temperature range to live in, enough air to breath etc. Absence of any of these will ensure the person's demise. Threaten this and the person is motivated to remove that threat e.g. they work to get money for food, they move to where water can be found, they wrap up well in the cold, they seek shade in the heat of the desert etc.

'**Safety and security**' needs are those which emanate from threats, or potential threats from the surroundings, such as theft, assault, attack by wild animals or people, tornadoes in the plain states of the USA. The threat of these will motivate people to support their local 'neighbourhood watch scheme', ask for more police on the block, fit their homes with locks, stay in their cars when driving through safari parks, not go down town alone and on foot after dark, carry a personal alarm or mobile phone, build tornado shelters in or under their homes etc.

'**Belonging needs**' are to do with the fact that the human race is a gregarious species and will normally suffer stress if alone for long periods (*solitary confinement is a punishment*). Once we are well fed and safe from attack then we seek the company of others for reasons other than safety in numbers. We are motivated to belong to a group: a family group, work group, occupational groups and clubs. Groups abound. In some cultures this drive can be so strong that people define themselves by their groupings, e.g. where they work, what club they belong to, their old school, their nation etc.

The need for '**esteem and status**' is an expression of the fact that people have a need to be needed. Once they belong to a group they must have a role within that group. It is not sufficient to just belong to a family, a person must have a position (*in the hierarchy*) within that family, e.g. mother, or father, uncle or aunt, eldest or youngest child etc. The more extended the family, the more important becomes the role a person may occupy. The same thing happens with clubs, such positions as club treasurer, secretary, chairperson, etc. confer status and importance and are sought out and contested during elections. This is what is referred to by the phrase 'the pecking order'.

'**Self actualisation**' is about a person making their own statement, to attempt to leave their mark on the world – in the extreme: to be a great artist, writer, scientist, round the world sailor etc. Most people will get their self-fulfilment from more mundane, but to them still very important things, such as gardening,

DIY, model making, dress making, being an entrepreneur starting and running their own successful business, making lots of money etc. (*not for the wealth so much as for the statement that this will make about them, to themselves*).

For any motivation to have sway, all the others lower in the hierarchy must be securely satisfied, in-place, forming a sound foundation on which to build. If any of the underlying needs are threatened then the superstructure comes tumbling down. It is difficult to imagine Mozart being able to compose 'Eine kleine nachtmusik' whilst being pursued alone in winter through the primeval forest by a sabre toothed tiger, his mind will be on survival – not actualisation.

Any product can be viewed as satisfying one or more of these motivations, the more of these that are encompassed then the more the product is secure against swings in the economic climate. e.g. food and clothing will always have a market, albeit that when times are tough they will be more basic that when there is money about. Markets for fine dining, continental holidays etc. will almost certainly suffer in a recession.

In business to business markets

In addition to the Maslow motivations* organisations have buying motives to do with the success of the business. These are part of a company's hierarchy of objectives so that:

- to make the desired return on capital,
- costs must be shaved from production,
- that requires a more productive machine,
- which in turn means that the customer has to buy that product.

Key Management Concept

* (*it is people who do the buying, and a buying motive in a business could be 'survival' i.e. keeping one's job by not buying a risky proposition. The strap line: 'no one ever got fired for buying IBM' illustrates this in action*).

These business to business needs can be usefully categorised into one of three classifications:

- those that are 'mission critical'
- those that are 'cull test' issues, important but not critical, and
- those that are nice to have, but not important.

'**Mission critical**' needs, if not satisfied will lead to the company failing to achieve some critical part of its business strategy.

'**Cull test**' needs are about the basic indispensable requirements. A vendor company's ability to satisfy these needs will enable them to be included (or not) on the short list of possible suppliers, i.e. the invitation to tender goes out to these companies only. Such needs may include the ability to:

- provide access to finance
- provide training for the buyers employees
- deliver when required etc.

'**Nice to have**' needs are such aspects of the product as colour, style, designer label etc.

As can be seen the importance of each of these will depend on the circumstances of the company, e.g. 'nice to haves' may be 'mission critical' for some and 'cull test' for others.

Whichever type of needs are addressed, it should be remembered that the customer buys to satisfy them via the benefits conferred by the product. These benefits derive from the 'features' of the product, e.g. the road holding of a tyre is conferred from the width, tread pattern and construction of that tyre (*i.e. cross ply or radial*); the ability to run an accounts package on a PC depends on the speed of the chip, the amount of RAM memory, the resolution of the screen and the size of the hard disk.

Sales people often explain their product's benefits to the customer by means of the acronym FAB, i.e. **F**eatures lead to – **A**dvantages which lead to – **B**enefits. Nowadays marketers will grab the attention of their audience by mentioning the benefits first, then explain how these are derived from the features and advantages of the product e.g. 'live an active old age' – via the benefits conferred by a daily pill replete with lots of vitamins and minerals and 'ginkgo bolover'.

Activity No. 2

Activity

The following is part one of the exercise for this chapter, we will start it now and complete it after the next section. This can be done for consumer or business to business markets. To do this exercise you will have to think of a typical important customer for your business.

The rows in Figure 2.4 page 70 have been labelled to indicate their importance.

For 'mission critical'

What are the two or three issues which are indispensable if your customer is to derive what they want from your product and thus reach their goal/s?

For 'cull test'

What are the minimum two or three essentials you need to have for the customer to even look at you?

For 'nice to haves'

What are the extras which are not critical for the customer to achieve their aims? They probably would not pay more to have them, but like bundled software for a PC, may well increase the customer's perception of value obtained.

Write these issues in their respective rows before moving on to the next section of this chapter:

Category of need	◄─────────── What these needs are ───────────►
Mission critical	
Cull test	
Nice to have	

Figure 2.4: Categorise your customers' needs

The main issue of this exercise is to discover how well you know your customer's needs, particularly for the 'mission critical' and 'cull test' aspects. Do you really know them? How do you know you know? Is this based on sound information or have you only guessed at them? Perhaps this will prompt you to do some real investigation into your customers' motives for buying.

The competitive differential advantage

Relationship building with key customers depends on a lot more than selling. Even in marriage the power of love can be strained if basic tangible benefits are not evident. The customer continuously needs a solid justification for preferring you as a supplier – a competitive advantage has to be perceived.

Competitive advantage can be created in one or a combination of two ways:

1. **Cost leadership**. This is obtained from production efficiencies, economies of scale, use of resources, value engineering and/or constant attention to driving down costs (*i.e. Kaizen as in Chapter 1*). This will enable the supplier to lead market pricing and, if necessary, beat those who erode the key customer base by price cutting. Because we are all part of a much longer value chain, which is only as strong as its weakest link, for the chain to compete effectively in highly competitive industries, members of the chain must realise that they have to help each other. The supplier's cost leadership, if reflected in their prices, enables their customer to be the cost leader in the customer's marketplace.

2. **Distinctive competence**. These are skills such as being good at innovation/responsiveness to customer needs, demonstrated by frequent small, but customer-driven improvements. And, as a consequence the package offered is distinctively more advantageous than that from your competitor. Being a 'preferred supplier' places a company in a unique position to monitor and respond promptly to the customer's changing needs and to set the benchmark of performance by which any competitive marauder will be judged.

It is necessary for suppliers to position themselves according to their customers' needs as above. In turn, these are determined by issues that are of technical and financial significance to them.

So, the question is: does the supplier go for cost leadership or distinctive competence to gain the edge?

A cost leadership strategy

If cost leadership is to be the chosen strategic thrust, it is essential for marketers to understand the cost infrastructure of both their customers and their own company. The aim is to provide acceptable quality at the lowest possible delivered cost and to use that cost efficiency to deter competitors from engaging in price-cutting and/or penetration strategies. To these ends, it is vital for the marketer to understand the main leverage points for cost advantage for the customer's industry, in general and for the customer in particular.

In professional services, attracting and keeping the best quality human resources assumes a significant proportion of the costs, but is critical to the quality of the performance. Full utilisation of these human resources and making sure that all their time is appropriately invoiced, is a key success factor. In addition, with high sales and marketing costs, a company should be targeting high frequency automatic repeat business, rather than the one-off short project that will probably require just as much time to sell and negotiate. The customer's cost structure will determine the degree of importance attached to the company's offering (good or service).

To be the cost leader supplier, the marketer must know what that competitors' costs are. For many manufacturing companies, the most obvious route to this information is to buy their competitors' product, strip it down and evaluate the cost (*which is common practice*). Indeed, studying the competition is now a mainstream activity to the extent that many companies regularly run recruitment campaigns for the express purpose of securing business intelligence from those applicants who work for rival concerns.

A value-driven strategy

This means achieving a superior value by serving customers' needs better than your competitors. Five issues have to be addressed:

1. Who is the customer? (We have to understand the customer's decision-making unit and identify exactly who we have to convince of the value of our products or services.)

2. What values are the decision makers seeking?

3. Will these customers perceive these values and be prepared to pay a premium for them?

4. Can our company deliver these values more effectively than the competition?

5. How can our company enhance its position and achieve superior value?

Key Question

In business to business customer-perceived value consists of benefits that increase gross profit by:

- improving performance
- reducing operating costs
- reducing working capital needs
- reducing risk

or reduce the investment cost of a product over its life cycle by:

- lowering purchase prices
- lowering installation and set-up costs
- lowering maintenance costs
- lowering financing costs
- lowering disposal costs

It is essential that the marketer fully understands some of the pitfalls of going for the value-driven option. These include:

- creating differences that buyers do not value

- pricing in excess of values delivered

- failure to understand the real cost of differentiation (*and not building it into the price*)

- looking only to the 'core product'* as the basis of differentiation and ignoring intangible aspects of service and support. (*See Chapter 4, Part I.)

Action Checklist

This latter point is especially important. With familiarity, the customer becomes accustomed to the special levels of service that are provided and they can often lose appreciation of the privileges that the relationship, as a preferred customer, imparts.

So the marketer must continue to remind their customers of the costs and benefits of the less visible aspects of their relationship and to continually re-sell their competitive advantage.

Key Management Concept

How to develop competitive advantage

Advantages can be developed by either competitor-based thinking or by customer-based thinking.

The competitor-based strategy is geared to superior quality, innovative technology, broader distribution, wider product ranges, superior technical service, better reputation and image.

A customer-based strategy is geared to customer problem solving, which may include improved reliability, lower operating costs, faster response, one-stop shopping or quality assurance. The difference is how the marketer measures the advantage – against the yardstick of competitor performance or against the benchmark of current customer productivity.

There are four steps to brainstorming competitive advantage:

1. Identify alternative advantage positions.

2. Screen the options – are they:

    •   meaningful – could the customer perceive the advantage?

    •   credible – would the customer believe the advantage (*given our past performance and reputations*)?

    •   unique, relative to the competition?

    •   contributing to our long-term objectives?

3. Select the option, making sure that the organisation understands and commits to deliver the advantage.

4. Finally, design the programmes to implement. Then identify the key success factors critical to the achievement and delivery of the perceived competitive advantage.

Success is determined by how clearly the customer can define how one company differs from its competitors, i.e. how does the customer complete the simple words that complete the phrase 'you are the ones who…'

Texas Instruments and Hewlett Packard are good examples of companies with strategic profiles at almost opposite ends of the spectrum. Over the years Texas Instruments, in large standard markets, has aimed for competitive advantage based on a long-production run low-cost position. Their targets are to achieve high volumes with a low price achieved via the cost-driven manufacturing experience curve. Their finances are aggressively resourced and extended. The people are competitive and motivated by individual incentives.

In contrast, Hewlett Packard focus on selected small markets based on unique, high-value products that are designed for performance. They are financially conservative with no debt. The team concept is of prime importance and is reflected in the format of their bonus schemes.

Hewlett Packard's growth has been controlled, whereas Texas Instrument's early rapid growth was based upon the total belief in 'motoring down the experience curve', whilst pursuing an R & D programme to turn aspirations of high volume economies of scale into a reality.

Market share

Well-documented research such as Profit Impact of Market Strategy (PIMS), establishes a strong correlation between market share and higher returns on investment (ROI), although nobody is quite sure whether it is market share that helps profit or profitability that helps to promote market share.

But whatever the reason, those companies that already have a strong market position possess a unique and valuable advantage. This should not be frittered away like so many other companies have done in the past (e.g. IBM, Triumph Motorcycles, the Co-op Retail Societies etc).

Remember: **Success** ▷ **Complacency** ▷ **Vulnerability** ▷ **Failure**.

Activity

Activity No. 3

We will now conclude the exercise started on page 69. Just as you envisaged a particular type of customer before, now identify a product (*or product range*) that your company offers this customer (*or type of customer*), and one which is designed to address as many needs as possible. Then identify a particular competitor (*the one who gives you the most concern*) who has similar products offered to the same customers, (*or types of customer*) as does your company.

This part of the exercise is to take each of the needs identified above, (*particularly the 'mission critical' or 'cull test'*) and examine how well your company's product satisfies these needs compared to how well the competitor's product does this.

- If you are better than the competitor then list the product in the relevant row under the column indicated with the plus sign (*i.e.*+).

- If you are equal, the product should be situated in the equals column (*i.e.*=).

- And if the competitor's product is better than yours, then show it under the minus sign (*i.e.*−).

Category of need	+	=	−
Mission critical			
Cull test			
Nice to have			

Figure 2.5: How do I compare versus the competition?

All the products that are not in the '+' column should cause you concern, the most concern being for those that are in the '−' column. The aim must be to move these to the left by addressing the customer's needs better than the competitor.

It is foolish to guess about these issues. You really must have confidence in what you 'know'. Unsubstantiated opinions are no basis for investment. There is only one way to really know how you perform versus the competitor, go ask the customer.

Marketing planning

The job of the marketing plan is effectively to deliver the company's competitive advantage to the marketplace so that the company can exploit this profitably. We look at the form of the marketing plan and the process to create one in more detail in Chapter 5. However, a brief examination of the relevance of the marketing plan will complete the introduction to how marketing works.

There are five main parts to the marketing plan:

1. The marketing audit, sometimes called the SWOT.

2. The strategy re. the sources of business and how these are to be gained in the face of competition.

3. The marketing mix to be used, detailing policies for each element.

4. The marketing programme (a sort of time and event schedule).

5. The monitoring and measurement strategies, policies, and practices to be employed.

And all of this is in pursuit of gaining market share, to be a dominant player in the market served.

The purpose of the marketing plan is to:

- decide on the policies for each of the elements of the marketing mix as described above

- generate a programme of events, that will focus and co-ordinate activities to realise these policies

- communicate these activities and allocate the various responsibilities to those who will be tasked with carrying out the plan i.e. who will do what, by when, with what resources (budgets etc.) and how success will be measured, and lessons learned for next time.

'The ability to learn faster than competitors (and act more quickly) may be the only sustainable competitive advantage (in the future)'.

Aire de'Gouse – Royal Dutch Shell

And that's the job of the market researcher which we will be examining later in Chapter 7.

Choosing your customers

Chapter 3

'If you are not segmenting – you are not marketing'
Professor Theodore Levitt, Harvard.

As marketing is all about 'a dialogue over time with a specific group of customers' (*i.e. getting closer to customers*), the critical first step is to define quite clearly who the customers will be and where the company will find them. Some marketers express this as their 'sources of business', in the sense that these are the companies and/or the people from whom they generate their income.

The process of defining one's source (*or sources*) of business has two stages:

  i)   deciding which markets are to be served

  ii) defining which particular group/s of customers within those markets will be addressed in particular (*segmentation*).

Market selection

As we have said in the previous chapter, it is of critical importance for the marketer to select the right market/s for the company's business. Get the right market and the company could flourish, get the wrong market and even with ten times the effort the company could die. There are two types of decisions – they are not mutually exclusive – when evaluating a market.

The two types of decisions are:

'Is it worthwhile to stay in the company's current market?'

i.e. is the grass greener in other markets. Or:

'Which new market should the company enter?'

The issues to weigh-up are:

- What is the market worth now?

- What could it be worth in the future?

- Where is the market on its life cycle ?

- How competitive will the company be in the new market? (*i.e. how potent is its CDA [competitive differential advantage], and what is the company's potential market share?*)

- What are the barriers to entry (*old and new markets*)?

Taking each of these issues in turn:

What is the market worth now?

A large sized market is not necessarily the most attractive. The larger and more valuable the cake the greater may be the competition, both in number and intensity. Competition always means higher costs of sale, therefore lower margins. In such large markets it nearly always pays to segment so as to avoid taking on the competition.

How competitive will the company be in the new market?

(*i.e. What is the company's potential market share?*)

The ability to compete depends on such issues as:

- The company's size – i.e. how much muscle can it bring to bear, how deep are its pockets in the face of a costly struggle etc.

- The extent to which its competitive differential gives it an advantage. (*see Chapter 2*)

The larger a company's market share, the greater the chance that it can be a price maker.

The smaller its market share, the greater the chance that the company will be a price 'taker' (*i.e. large companies put a glass ceiling on what their smaller competitors can charge*).

What could the market be worth in the future?

(*i.e. is the company's potential market share going to be worth much?*)

Growing markets always seem the most attractive, it is human nature to want to catch the wave that will carry the company successfully into the future. For the 'early birds' this can lead to much success. However, the determinant of success is spotting the wave before the herd, when the conditions are at their least competitive. This gives the company time to establish itself before the market becomes fashionable. Once the herd starts to move into this new market the level of competitive intensity rises, and it becomes severe during the mature stage of the product life cycle (*see Chapter 1*).

Where is the market on its life cycle?

As we have said above, most companies see the potential of a market as being greatest during its growth phase. This may be true in terms of sheer volume, but frequently not so in terms of profitability.'Often there is gold at the end of the rainbow!' – for those who know where to look and how to exploit it. It is in the latter decline stage of a life cycle that the competition will often be at its least, which means margins can more easily be maintained.

Two examples, will serve to illustrate:

The Morris Minor Centre, originally established itself in Bath. When the Morris Minor, and its variants were finally discontinued by the British Motor Company. This centre provided owners with sources of spare parts, access to repairs and to other owners. The car was much loved by many of its owners who were reluctant to abandon it to some scrap heap. The Morris Minor is now seen by some as being a classic car, and the Morris Minor Centre made a fortune.

The Classic Connection Ltd specialise in supplying and fitting the appropriate tyres to vintage and classic cars. These vehicles are owned as investments. However, few of them are squirrelled away in museums never to see the light of day. Often these cars are driven during rallies and other social events for the sheer enjoyment, so the tyres wear out. The Classic Connection has acquired most of the moulds in which tyres for these cars are made. Most of the owners of these classic and vintage vehicles are very wealthy, owning these cars is a self indulgence for them. Thus, exploiting the law of supply and demand (*see Chapter 1*) Classic Connection can almost charge what they like. This company is also very profitable.

What are the barriers to entry, (old and new markets)?

Barriers to entry discourage new companies from entering a market. The relevance of this depends on whether the company in question is an incumbent or a potential new entrant. If an incumbent, then whatever barriers exist are seen as lessening the chances of having to face unwanted competition. Like the walls of a mediaeval town, they protect the market from the invader. For a potential new entrant, these 'walls' have to be scaled, and to do so, even if possible, may be too costly. Some examples of barriers to market entry are, market structure, technology, marketing spend by the incumbents, the law etc.

Key Question

Market structure is an indicator of competitive intensity. It is to do with the ratio of the numbers of incumbent companies to the volume/value of business they do. A market is said to be highly structured when 20% or less of the companies in a market account for 80% of the value of the business in that market. If this is the case, there are some big muscular and rich competitors with whom the invader may have to fight.

Key Management Concept

An unstructured or fragmented market is one where the above ratios are reversed, i.e. it takes more than 20% of the companies in a market to do 80% of its business. The more unstructured a market the less intense the competition, in the sense that rather than having to face one big adversary there will be many small ones but none of them with the resources to put the new entrant out of the market. Also, the incumbents will probably be under fire themselves, they may not have the time or inclination to attack, the chances are they may not even notice the extra competitor or two, so one more in the market is not going to make much difference.

Key Management Concept

Technology can be an entry barrier to a market, especially if it is highly specialised and advanced – the rate of advance is an important factor. Any new entrant will need to discover ways to gain this technological expertise, and the faster the better. This will require either a great deal of money to catch up with the market leaders or to buy a company which is already at the 'state of the art'. If the market is highly structured the chances of being able to acquire such a portal into the market are very slim indeed, the big players will want to buy them first.

Marketing spend – incumbent companies can create barriers against new entrants by spending so much on advertising to establish their brands, that any company wishing to compete will have to match this spend in the long-run, but in the short-term, will have to spend a great deal more just to become noticed and established before they can hope to sell anything. A good example of this is the UK market for home laundry detergents. There are only two suppliers of branded products, Unilever and Proctor and Gamble, and they spend so much on promotion that any other company in the business can only market via the chain store's own label detergent, because there is no way they can afford to match the spending of the big two. And, unless they do, they will not be heard over the noise of promotion already in the market.

Key Management Concept

The law of the land apart from monopolies via patents, or via government fiat, the law can impose such restrictions on a market that the cost of compliance can cause a barrier. An example of this is the financial services industry, even Richard Branson had to partner an incumbent in the form of Norwich Union in order to establish Virgin Direct.

Segmentation

Segmentation is the application of the marketer's need to:

1. 'focus', so as to get closer to the customer and

2. 'outflank' the opposition. It is important for the marketer never to fight on the ground of the competitor's own choosing.

Taking the last point first:

On the basis that the larger the market share the greater the chance the company is a price *maker*, and the smaller the market share, the greater the chance the company is a price *taker*, companies that do not dominate the market find themselves having to consider a head-on confrontation with the major player in their market in order just to survive.

Key Learning Point

Market segmentation is a means of stepping out from underneath the dominance of otherwise market leaders. By redefining the marketplace in which the company operates the marketer targets those customers the opponent has neglected.

Put simply, segmentation is the process of:

- Dividing a market into smaller, more homogeneous groups of customers **on the basis of the customers' needs**.

- Selecting from these groups those which the marketer believes:

   a) have needs which so far are not properly addressed ('gap in the market')

   b) his/her company can address them to the improved satisfaction of customers ('competitive differential advantage')

   c) the sub group is large enough to be profitable for his/her company ('market in the gap')

The company can establish effective communications and address each group selected with a marketing mix unique to that group.

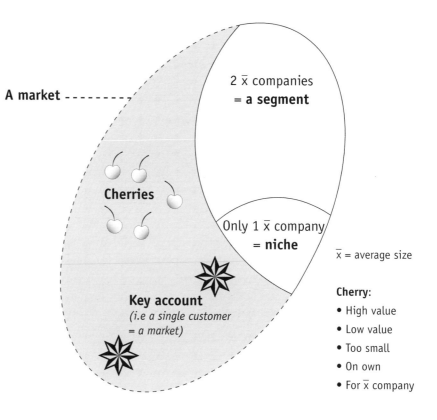

$\bar{x}$ = average size

Cherry:
- High value
- Low value
- Too small
- On own
- For $\bar{x}$ company

Figure 3.1: Segment variants

Segments come in a range of sizes. If a market is sliced into fairly large groups, where each group can support two or more average size suppliers, it is called a 'market segment'. If, however, those groupings are smaller and are only large enough to support one average size supplier, then it is referred to as a market 'niche'.

If the division goes smaller still, the name used is 'cherry picking'. Cherry picking is the practice of addressing small groups of 'high value – low volume business'. Cherry pickers present a considerable threat to the larger players (size and share) in most markets.

By segmenting a market, the company increases its understanding of its customers' needs, it improves its ability to identify market opportunities and provides a clearer idea of what strategies and implementable actions need to be taken. The process of segmenting effectively locks out the competition. Segments (cherry niche et al) are homogeneous in the sense that customers within that group have more in common between themselves when it comes to their behaviour towards the products in question, than they have with people in other segments. Marketers refer to this as 'intra-segment homogeneity' and 'inter-segment heterogeneity'.

Segment strategy approaches

A critically important task is the selection of the most appropriate number of target markets for the company to address and how, in general terms, to differentiate among them.

When several segments are attractive three broad strategy options are open to the company. These are known as:

- the **undifferentiated** strategy (i.e. not segmenting at all)
- the **concentration** strategy
- the **differentiated** strategy. See Figures 3.2, 3.3 and 3.4 following.

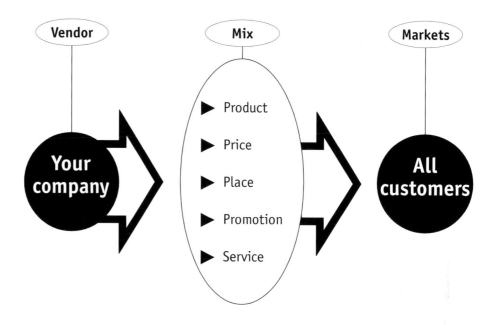

Figure 3.2: Undifferentiated strategy

Undifferentiated strategy

This approach offers the same mix to all the segments of the market. Since by definition the needs of each segment differ, it must fail. It maximises efficiency but minimises effectiveness. Some monopolists get away with this but it makes them vulnerable to future entrants.

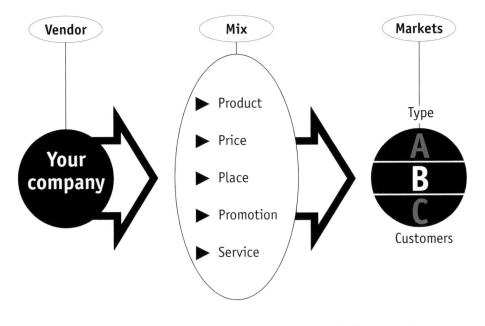

Figure 3.3: Concentration strategy

Concentration strategy

Here companies select the most attractive segment, and after researching needs and conditions in it, target their resources using a single tailored marketing mix. This approach loses economies of scale but enhances effectiveness. It has been applied successfully, for example, in the motor industry by Rolls Royce and Morgan, and Cray Super Computers in the IT industry.

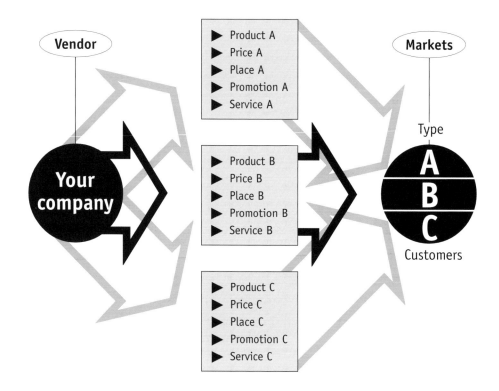

Figure 3.4: Differentiated strategy

Differentiated strategy

Here the company targets multiple attractive segments with each mix appropriately adapted to fit each segment. It gives some scope for scale and raises effectiveness. General Motors is a good exponent of this strategy in the car business, or Seiko in watches.

How to segment

As we have seen the three conditions necessary for a segmentation strategy to succeed, are that:

- there must be a 'gap in the market', in the sense that there are customers that have **needs** which are not currently being satisfied (*to the extent which we believe is possible*). This is where the successful marketers will start their search.

The second issue is that:

Action Checklist

- there must be a 'market in that gap' in the sense that the chosen group of customers is large enough to be viable and warrant the investment necessary.

Finally:

- the company must be able to communicate with that segment in the full sense of the word. Can they research it, promote to it, deliver to it? (*i.e. two way, and in terms of the full marketing mix*).

It is important to note that all three conditions must be present simultaneously. If any are missing, then that postulated segment is not a viable proposition.

The process

The various strategies for segmenting a market are presented by the cascade diagram, Figure 3.5 below.

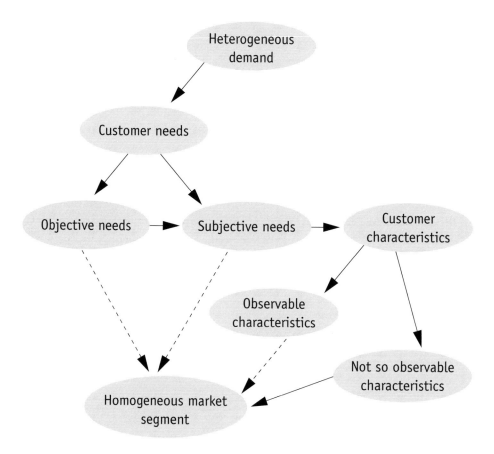

Figure 3.5: Segmenting a market

The 'cascade' (as shown by the arrows) is the 'process' by which a market is segmented. To separate out the different types of customer – one from the other

– discriminating variables must be used. For example, gender separates out and discriminates males from females. These variables are shown at the 'decision nodes' i.e. the shaded areas.

Stage one of the process commences with an analysis that searches for unfulfilled demand (*current or potential*). In other words, segments related to what the customers require and are willing to pay a 'profitable' price for, (*i.e. not just 'need' or 'want'*). These requirements can be sub-divided into objective needs versus subjective needs. Objective needs are those that can be measured to a commonly agreed standard, (*which for a service can only be 'time', see Chapter 2*).

If objective needs draw a blank the wise marketer will look toward subjective needs to define the potential segment.

One of the advantages of marketing a service related, or a service enchanced, product is that a given 'core' service has the potential to be almost all things to all customers. The very intangible nature of service means that, with the exception of time, all other evaluations of quality are subjective. Thus, the service marketer would look at such subjective issues as:

- the status

- the social visibility

- the amount of inter-personal service which clients want

- the political respectability (*e.g. does this bank exploit the poor in third world countries?*)

- the psychographic needs of the customer as expressed in the technology adoption curve (*see Figure 3.6, page 102*).

The marketer next identifies what types of customers exhibit these particular objective or subjective requirements, (*i.e. we now need to know who wants what*).

1. For the purposes of segmentation, customers can be described using two sets of criteria:

    • that which can easily be seen: for example, their 'observable characteristics' and

    • that which can't be so readily seen: for example, their 'non-observable characteristics'.

The easiest of these elements to examine are the observable characteristics, the definition of which any reasonably intelligent, fairly moderately educated person would be able to tell by looking.

In consumer markets, for example, the customer's:

    • age
    • gender
    • race
    • location
    • socio-economic class etc.

In other words their demography.

In business to business markets:

    • Are the customers large or small companies?

    • Are they in high-tech or low-tech, the service sector or manufacturing?

    • What sort of industry are they in, e.g. chemicals, utilities, agriculture?

The marketer should then proceed to examine customer characteristics for non-observable phenomena.

2. In a consumer market this will mainly be along the lines of the personality (*sometimes known as psychographics*) of the prospect. There are numerous ways of defining personality – many of them have proved useful when defining segments.

Additional variables in this category include people's opinions, beliefs, leisure activities, level of education etc. All of which are difficult to see at a glance but, with the right skills, can be used to segment.

In a business to business situation this might be 'company culture'. (The reader should also consider *Psychographics in Business to Business* as per *Crossing the Chasm* by Geoffrey A. Moore).

Whilst it is possible to form a viable segmentation strategy from just customer demand (*objective or subjective measures*), the more of these variables that are included in the definition of the market segment, the more stable that segmentation strategy becomes.

So, for example, a bank could identify that there was a type of small business which, because of the owner's lifestyle, required access to their money at all times of the day, and days of the week, particularly when banks were normally closed (*i.e. their objective needs*). This group of companies and the people running them, the bank knew, were highly sensitive to politically correct issues. They did not want to deal with a financial institution that exploited the third world, nor failed to give equal opportunities to race, religion or gender (*i.e. their subjective needs*). So far so good, but the financial service marketer now needs to know how to recognise these people/companies. The next stage therefore is to note that these needs, previously identified, are particularly prevalent amongst small software Value Added Resellers (VARs) specialising in customising Microsoft programmes for the smaller company in the retail sector. The 'entrepreneurs of these VARs are frequently male, highly socially mobile and members of local business networks such as the Chambers of Commerce, Rotarians, the 'Round Table' etc. (*i.e. their 'observable' characteristics*).

If we link all that together then we have a company foundation on which to build our segment. So, if these VARs were to be predominantly located near colleges of further education or universities the marketing strategy should ensure that an automatic teller machine were placed on every campus, whether the bank had an office there or not.

Additionally, the bank would run special promotions to these entrepreneurs via the social activities in which they participate and would employ dynamic PR to enhance and protect its 'acceptable' image to this group.

The types of market segmentation for consumer and business markets consist of:

Benefit segmentation alone, as we have discussed above.

Situation – the situation companies may find themselves in at a particular time, such as for example, a business traveller who needs to change travellers cheques after bank closing hours, is the ideal target market for Bureau de Change.

Psychographics segmentation is all about defining people by their personality. As there are over 650 personality traits this can become cumbersome to use, so what most marketers have done is to cluster these together into psychographic segments and put labels on them which will serve as short hand, (*such as 'yuppy' – young upwardly mobile urban professional. 'Woopy' – well-off older person, 'dink' – dual income, no children.* Personality is of tremendous importance when segmenting the market for an IT related service. (*See 'crossing the chasm' on page 102*).

Key Management Concept

Geographic segmentation exploits the location of the customer – wherever they may be.

Usage segmentation is about what the customer does with one's product. So for example, mobile phones can be used either for:

- incoming and outgoing calls whilst on the move (normal pattern?)

- outgoing calls only (trainers can't take calls in the seminar)

- data transmission (i.e. linked to notebook/laptop)

- any combination of the above: nationally only; internationally etc.

Segmentation in some business to business markets feature benefits such as company loyalty and buyers' motives, (*in other words the buyers previous purchase behaviour*). Therefore buyers in businesses are not just concerned with physically obtaining supply but also with making a statement about their buying abilities in the organisation, or playing a political game to guard themselves against future recrimination.

Suitable technology is also a means by which we can segment a business to business market, do our customers have the technology to be able to use our products? Someone marketing software packages designed for the intranet for example, would have to focus on those organisations that have the necessary hardware to carry that software's requirements.

The remaining segmentation types for locating business to business segments are:

> **'Type of end use'**, i.e. the actual use for the IT and/or service. For a vehicle maintenance supplier it may be to keep customers' vehicles on the road, via regular or preventative maintenance, or it could be to train people to operate a hotline for example.

The type of industry as a means of segmenting the market would address the service sector, rather than the manufacturing sector, local authority, rather than financial services and so forth.

The job function of the user – is the user a manager, a manual worker, a financial director, a designer etc?

Segmenting for services

The following section looks specifically at the focus of service market segmentation which must concentrate on three main areas:

- time
- people
- psychographics.

Key Management Concept

Time and the flavours of time. As a segmentation, variable time, for our purposes has five 'flavours':

- punctuality
- speed of response
- availability
- duration
- speed of innovation.

We can also usefully segment via our **process strategy** – such as the customer wishing to have their status confirmed or to have the service performed quickly and efficiently.

People – the type of people that are going to be served. So we cater to inter-customer influence.

Staff/customer harmony – i.e. do our people and the customer's staff get on very well together?

Resource – we might segment the market according to those we would want to take up our service during peaks, such as senior managers in multi-nationals, versus those we would wish to take up the service during slack time, such as small companies and junior managers and we would price and package our service accordingly.

The culture of an organisation and the lifestyles of the people in the company could well effect the way that a particular company should be treated as a customer. Lifestyle of course is a compound of four major areas: activities, interests, opinions and the demography. The demographic component is aimed specifically at helping us communicate with our target audience.

Segmenting for an IT related market

'Crossing the chasm'

Markets in the IT industry can often usefully be segmented by the psychographics associated with the diffusion of innovation. The diffusion of innovation curve has been known since the early 1920s via work on the adoption of technology amongst farmers throughout the world, both in America and also the under developed world.

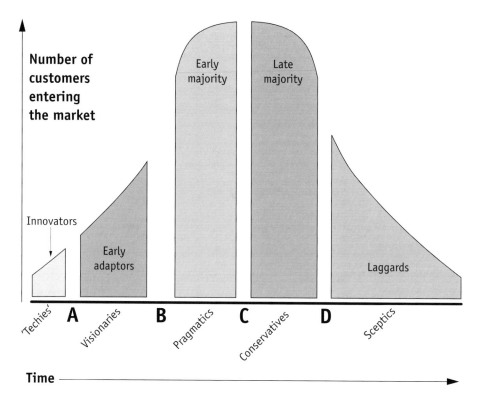

Figure: 3.6 Technology adoption curve – as a psychographic segmentation base

The 'curve' is a 'normal distribution' and illustrates what appears to be essential human behaviour. The 'mainstream' of the market being the early and late majority i.e. within one standard deviation each side of the mean (*in other words they represent 68% of the market.*) However, two standard deviations to the left of the mean will include the 'early adopters' and three standard deviations will include 'innovators'. Two standard deviations to the right of the mean will encounter the 'laggards'. The main issue is that these are psychographic segments related to the buyer's perception of, and behaviour towards, risk.

Key Management Concept

In short, innovators love to be 'first on the block to amaze their friends'. In terms of the technology industry, innovators (*in the form of 'Techies'*) take great delight in exploring new technologies merely to see if it works.

Early adopters are the visionaries. To convince early adopters you need to be able to show that the innovation has a practical application to their business from which they can benefit.

The early majority, (*34% of the total market*) want to climb on board the band wagon only when the major products (*goods or services*) can clearly be identified.

The 'late majority' are much more risk averse and they will only adopt the innovation when it is well proven and easy to use along such lines as the graphic user interface (G.U.I. i.e. Windows) for example.

Finally the laggards, who abhor any innovation and any change. They will only 'adopt' if the innovation is heavily disguised within the products that they are currently buying. For example, nowadays they can't really avoid buying microprocessors when they buy cars or washing machines. However, if Laggards are a significant part of the market – the presence of microprocessors is not stressed.

Between each of these major groups there are psychological gaps (*chasms*) that need to be crossed. The gaps between innovators and early adopters, between the early majority and the late majority and between the late majority and the laggards, are only half (as big as) the distance that has to be crossed between early adopters and the early majority. This is the true chasm.

This model not only suggests a very powerful way of segmenting a market for services in any technology related business, but it also strongly recommends strategies for crossing these particular gaps and particularly the 'chasm' between the early adopters and the early majority. It is particularly useful when considering market development for technological goods and services. The types of goods affected include new forms of processor or computer screen, or overhead projector tablet etc. However, for the service aspect of marketing technology, the concept is absolutely critical because it not only indicates how the service marketer can get their technology related service adopted in the marketplace, but also where service can be used to add further value (to either goods or other services).

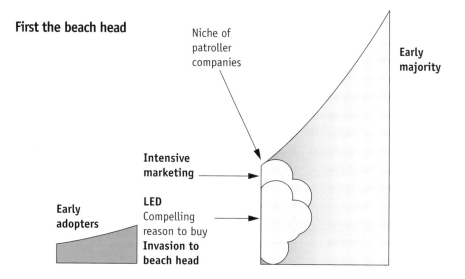

Figure 3.7a: Strategy for crossing the chasm

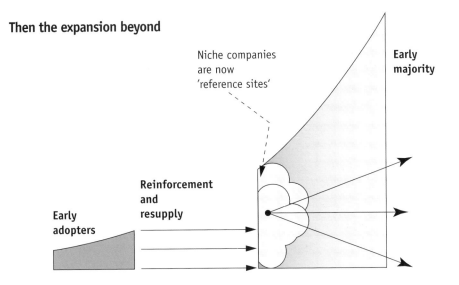

Then the expansion beyond

Niche companies are now 'reference sites'

Early majority

Reinforcement and resupply

Early adopters

Figure 3.7b: Strategy for crossing the chasm

When crossing the major 'chasm', the strategy of the cherry picker or the niche marketer is recommended. The innovating company needs to obtain strong references amongst the early majority or they will have absolutely no chance of success in the future. This major part of the market (early majority) contains a subset which are referred to as 'patrollers'. Their job is to patrol the chasm and ensure that no hair brain schemes make the crossing. 'Patrollers' tend to be large companies that are well respected amongst the rest of the early majority. They must be identified, targeted and converted in that initial invasion, otherwise without that beachhead the innovating company has little, if any, chance of diffusing innovation throughout the mainstream of the marketplace.

Having once established the bridgehead with a significant niche of the early majority patrollers, they can then be used as a stepping stone to create the breakout in various directions as the opportunities arise.

Establishing the initial beachhead is very much a marketing led, highly intensive sales invasion of the patroller's niche. Moving out from this beachhead reverts to a sales led marketing operation with the patrollers being used to establish leads and provide references to convert the remainder of this most important and very profitable mainstream segment (see *Crossing the Chasm* and *Inside the Tornado* by Geoffrey A. Moore).

Final principle

Action Checklist

To conclude this section on segmentation, it is important to note four basic principles of segmentation:

i)   It is always more effective to use several variables rather than just one.

ii) There is a trade-off – between the desire to know and the cost of obtaining that information, i.e. principle of the law of diminishing returns.

iii) Market segmentation and product differentiation are **joint** decisions but it is also important not to forget that a segmentation strategy involves the whole marketing mix. Thus, not just the product will be differentiated, but also the price, the promotion, the physical evidence, the process, the distribution and, in the service industry the people who are delivering the service during the moments of truth.

iv) The largest market segment is not always the most desirable. Many companies have made a lot of money out of looking for small segments (cherry pickers, niche players) sometimes even at the end of their life cycles. The larger companies stay away because they often believe these small and perhaps declining markets represent very little opportunity i.e. for them there is no market in the gap. This leads to less competition which means that there is also little price competition and thus profitability can be very healthy indeed.

Activity No. 4

Although useful to all businesses the following exercise is essential for those readers who previously classed their companies products no better than the competition (*i.e. situated them within columns '=' or '–' in Activity 3, Chapter 2*).

'Gap in the market'

Refer to the customer needs considered in Activity 3, Chapter 2 (page 76):

1. Select a specific set of one or two special customer needs that are mission critical to the customers who have them (i.e. these needs are important to a subset of the customers in the market), and that the benefits from your competitors' offerings do not adequately satisfy:

Then:

i) Spell out what they are

ii) Classify each as to whether they are objective or subjective needs.

The needs	Objective/subjective

Now, for the **'market in the gap'**. (*Here you will most probably need to do some research, read Chapter 7 to find out how.*)

2. Specify, which particular characteristics describe these customers, and from these select those which also differentiate them from other customers in the market. This differentiation/discrimination is critical – you are trying to segregate your customers from the 'herd' – if you can't do that you can't address your mix to them specifically.

   i)   Spell out what these are.

   ii) Classify them as to observable or non-observable.

The special characteristics	Observable/non-observable

3. Enumerate how many of these customers there are in the market.

4. Put a value on them in total.

   A simple way to do this is to:

   a) Estimate what the average value per customer purchase would be, then multiply this by:

   –   the number of times each would purchase per year, then

   –   the average number of years a company could expect to keep these customers if they were looked after well, and finally by

   –   the numbers of customers in the segment.

   State the product of the above £ _____ millions/thousands.

5. **Is this value worth the investment in time and effort**? (*i.e. either as straight profit or as a stepping stone to others in a cherry picking strategy, OR as a block to stop your competition getting a toehold in your market etc.*)

    If still no, then go back to item No.1. and start again. If yes to any of the above, proceed to discover:

    How best can you communicate?

6. **Research**:

    –   What media do they consume? (*i.e. not just read, but also believe, internalise and act upon*),

    –   Are there databases, mailing (*or other types of*) lists available to buy or hire?

    –   How many browse the Internet? How frequently?

State these, and if you can do so with confidence (*it's your money*) you have defined a segment/niche, or cherry.

NOTE: In some cases in business to business markets it is often possible to go through the whole exercise with only one major customer – this will be a key account. However, that's another topic entirely.

The marketing mix

The product

....

Chapter 4: Part I

What 'products' are

In everyday speech it is usual to talk of 'products' or 'services'. The implication being that the tangibles are products and the intangibles are services. However, at this point, for the sake of clarity and usefulness we must be more pedantic.

As intimated in Chapter 2, the customer does not so much buy products, as buy what those products will do for them or their company. They buy what the marketer sells because of what they can get out of it, not necessarily what the company puts in. And what is 'got out' is known as the product's 'benefits'(*or its 'satisfactions' depending on which author you read*).

These 'benefits' derive from the features the company puts in so that 'goods', such as cookware, cars, writing paper etc. have features that offer benefits. 'Services', such as training, legal advice, package holidays etc. also have features that offer benefits – as set out below:

Item	**One feature – providing...**	**One benefit** (*of several*)
Goods		
• cookware	• nonstick surface	• easy to clean
• car	• hatch-back	• easy access to load space
• writing paper	• water mark	• a status letterhead
Services		
• training	• short courses	• less loss of productivity via time away
• legal advice	• contingency fee (i.e. no win-no fee)	• affordable risk
• package holiday	• guaranteed sun	• impressive tan

Nowadays, many products are a collection of both goods and services, for example when someone buys a PC, this gains its benefits both from:

Goods

The size of the screen (*feature*) makes it easier to read (*benefit*), the speed of the chip (*feature*) makes it faster and thus saves time (*benefits*).

Services

Delivery, installation, and speed of doing so (*feature*) gets it up and running without hassle (*benefit*), training and hotline support (*feature*) helps the buyer get the best out of the machine (*benefit*): on-site and speedy maintenance (*feature*) helps the machine to be more productive and for longer (*benefit*).

Because both goods and services yield benefits, and today they are frequently sold in combination, it is more useful for the marketer to think of the product as being the bundle of benefits on offer, what some people refer to as the 'offering', be these benefits derived from goods, services or a combination of the two.

If necessary the marketer can always be more specific by referring to goods, if the offering is a 'tangible' and services if not.

This protocol, where the word 'product' stands for the total benefits on offer, from wherever derived, will be adhered to in the text that follows.

When a marketer designs a product to offer to the market (*goods or services*) he/she will consider first what are the customer needs to be addressed. What benefits will satisfy these needs and thus what features the product design should contain so as to deliver these benefits. The good marketer will employ this process of product definition, in the order above.

The total product concept

It is also very useful to classify the features and benefits of any one product along the lines suggested by the following model proposed by Theodore Levitt (*theory of the product life cycle*). This model is known by various names and is interpreted in as many different ways. However, for our purposes the author offers the following which his experience has found most useful.

Key Management Concept

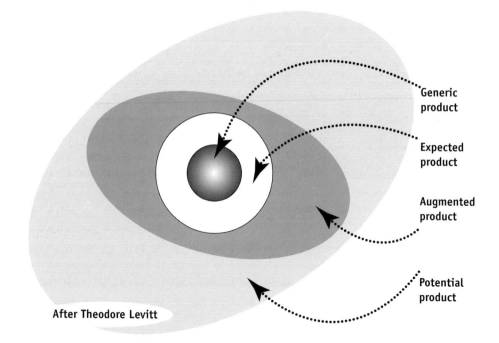

Generic product

Expected product

Augmented product

Potential product

After Theodore Levitt

Figure 4.1: The Levitt Concept

In this model the product can usefully be considered to consist of three layers, each founded on those closer to the middle. The product's future is the reservoir of ideas which surrounds all three. This has no boundary, it is limited only by the company's collective imagination.

To describe, illustrate and reveal the relevance of each part of the product in turn:

Generic or core

This is the heart and the foundation of the product. The generic is both internal to the company and to the product itself. It consists of all those things a company must do in order to get the product to offer the features that will yield the benefits required.

For goods such as a car, it could include the zinc galvanisation of the under body, both zinc coated metal and the process that deposits the zinc. This 'galvanisation' is a feature which confers less rust, longer body shell life and thus the benefit of the vehicle maintaining its value longer.

For a service business such as an airline it is everything the company must do to get the plane operational including:

- Training all the crew – both air crew, cabin crew, airside and landside crew etc.

- At the end of a flight, and before the next – emptying all the tanks that need to be emptied, and filling all those that should be full.

- Servicing the engines regularly, ensuring the landing gear tyres have no bald patches etc.

It also involves the operational process necessary to get the passengers on to the plane with their luggage.

- Taking the bookings

- Managing the check-in for passengers and their luggage

- Shepherding them on to the plane at the appropriate time etc.

Some commentators believe that the 'generic' comprises more than 70% of everything that the company does to bring about the product. And yet, done well, the generic is often invisible to the customer. The same commentators say that it directly contributes less than 11% of the satisfactions that a customer derives from the product – mainly because whatever skills and processes are involved they are beyond the customers' willingness or skills to evaluate. Because of this the 'generic' is, and should be, so much in the background that customers take it for granted. Yet the quality of the generic is vital. It stays in the background only so long as things go well. When things go wrong, even though that mishap may be trivial, it can have a dramatic impact on the customer's perception of the quality of the total product. As a former airline CEO once said '...*if the seat tray in front of the passenger is dirty with coffee stains from several flights ago, and is wobbly because some screws are missing, they can be excused for believing that this is the way we service our engines*'.

Without a well founded generic no 'total' product can be built.

Expected (or hygiene factor, or cull test)

Key Learning Point

Customers feel qualified to judge this aspect. Any absence of factors which go to make up the expected for them, can have a direct impact on their ability to enjoy the basic benefits from the product. For a car it could be the quality of the ride, the in-car entertainment, a large enough boot space, an automatic transmission etc. For the airline: it could be the times of the scheduled flights to the desired destination. Does the airline go direct or will passengers have to change flights at a 'hub', the speed of check-in, the reliability of the baggage handling etc.

Sometimes the 'expected' is referred to as either a 'hygiene factor' (*a term borrowed from Hertzberg's explanation of motivation*) or a cull test, in that the absence of the right factors here will ensure that the company is not short listed, it will not be invited to tender; or, current customers will leave if factors formerly present, are no longer provided.

Augmented (or competitive differential advantage)

Sometimes referred to as the 'product surround' this aspect of the product is 'motivational' (*from Hertzberg again*) in that it can cause customers to switch their business to this company.

Key Learning Point

The contents of this part of the product should provide benefits which uniquely satisfy customers, and do this better than the competitors products – in the perception of the customer – not just the marketer. The items that comprise the 'augmented product' should be aimed at the customers' 'mission critical' issues, as per the exercise in Chapter 2.

The benefits offered here, therefore, must be targeted at, and be specific to the intended customer. The acronym K.I.S.S (*'Keep it simple stupid' – we will encounter this again under promotion, Part IV*) is appropriate, because if there are too many benefits promoted the customer may not be able to identify those which are pertinent to them.

Examples of augmented factors are:

For the motor car

- Guaranteed buy-back at a guaranteed price.
- Air conditioning.
- It confers status in the driver's community.
- Side impact bars for safety – etc.

For the airline

- Limousine collection and delivery to the airport of departure and delivery to the destination at the other end.
- Larger more comfortable seats on long-haul flights.
- Power points for notebook computers in business class.
- Seat-back video screens etc.

The lists can go on – but note how each facet is easy to copy, one auto-manufacturer does it, and soon the rest will follow, it is the same with the airline examples. If an innovation gives a company an advantage, the others in the market would be negligent not to follow suit, or to try and leapfrog with a different innovation. And thus yesterday's augmentation can become an expected, a standard, a cull test, a hygiene item tomorrow.

The potential product (or reservoir of ideas)

Key Learning Point

As yesterday's differential rapidly becomes today's expected, in an increasingly competitive world, it is necessary to have the ability to stay one step ahead of the competition. The wise marketer, therefore, will constantly be collecting and evaluating ideas as to how to differentiate his/her product from all the sources they can.

It is the mark of a good entrepreneur that they are not too proud to borrow ideas from others. Often they will pass these off as their own ideas, which is plagiarism. The more capable will have no trouble giving source attribution, which is scholarship and thus honourable. Ideas can be had wherever one looks, keep cuttings, make notes (*Somerset Maugan's note books went for a fortune at auction, not just for the collector's value, but for the wealth of plot ideas*) no one ever knows when an idea will come in useful. However, it is the mark of a good marketer that they don't try to transpose these ideas into their own market, it may not be right in its raw state, it may require translation.

The author once consulted for a major department store. It was about the time that the phrase 'have a nice day' was first crossing the Atlantic. The client wished the floor staff of several stores to adopt the saying so as to see how well it would work in the UK. Typically customers were cynical, and the occasional few were openly derogatory – '*…and what's it to you!*' was one vehement remark which caused upset. One evening the author discussed this with a taxi driver. When the author finished his journey, the taxi driver wished the author a safe journey, said that he hoped to see him again soon, and asked the author to give the taxi driver's regards to Plymouth. Before handing the author the receipt for his fare, the taxi driver asked to be told what he had just said – after a short discussion in which the author was at a loss to answer to the taxi driver's satisfaction, the taxi driver declared that he was saying the equivalent of 'have a nice day' in English-English, as apposed to American-English, and by golly he was!

This makes the point beautifully – the marketer should never just transpose an idea into his/her market, they should know their market sufficiently to translate the idea (*i.e. into English-English*).

Key Learning Point

The marketer's strategy therefore must be to put in place a continuous programme expressly for the generation, evaluation and 'banking' of ideas.

Marketers should read widely, particularly the business and trade press, (but should not be confined to them). Including, in business to business markets management walking about (MBWA), occasionally accompanying sales people when they visit customers, these are a most powerful way for a marketer to keep in touch with the market (*better than any paper report*).

In consumer markets, there is little that provides better results than regular focus group discussions with customers and consumers (*see Chapter 7*).

The following two examples of potential ideas come from many years of running focus group discussions with customers of taxi companies and patients of medical practices. Some of these ideas are:

For taxi companies

- Payment by credit card (*now very common in the USA, in some places it is an 'expected' – a true cull test. Airline passengers will frequently not use cabs that don't accept credit cards*).

- Loyalty schemes for regulars (*air miles in some cases*).

- Choice of music for longer journeys.

- A rack of today's papers close to the passenger.

- Cell-phone for passenger use, paid for with the fare or by credit card.

- Lady drivers for lady passengers, particularly after dark etc.

For a medical practice

- Refreshments in the waiting room, tea, coffee etc. (*a practice in north Somerset serves wine in the evenings according to the Times 11 November 1996*).

- Very early (*6am*) and very late (*9pm*) surgeries to serve those who commute to work.

- A creche for the patient's children.

- Public telephone facilities (*not everyone has a mobile*).

- The doctor comes to the waiting room to greet patients.

- Consulting rooms on mainline rail terminuses, etc.

Ideas so gathered should be evaluated, and if they prove they have potential, should be stored in readiness for the day that the competitor either copies the current competitive differential, or betters it.When that happens, the appropriate new idea should be brought into action with ultimate speed, so as to ensure that the competition has little chance to gain a lead by exploiting their (temporary) parity or advantage.

Ideas in the category 'potential' should be stored in such a way that they are regularly, and not too infrequently, dusted off, and updated. There is usually not enough time to do this when their presence in the marketplace is required.

The total product concept has enormous beneficial impact on the potential profitability of the product. Factors that 'augment' the product form the basis for value added pricing' (*see the next section in this chapter, i.e. Part II pricing*).

Activity

Activity No. 5

Deconstruct the product that you addressed in Chapter 2, Exercise 2, and in Chapter 3. Say what you believe to be the relevant facets of:

The generic product i.e. the necessary +70% that makes up the 'generic' part of the product which customers don't care about until it goes wrong.

_____

_____

_____

_____

The expected product i.e. the minimum the product must have to be acceptable. What the customers feel capable to judge you by.

_____

_____

_____

_____

Now **the augmented product** – what does actually give you a competitive advantage? What will make customers come to you, stay with you, wait for you, and hopefully pay more for your product?

_____

_____

_____

_____

Now brainstorm to discover all the ways, no matter how fanciful, whereby you can provide a competitive advantage in the future, in other words build a list of the factors that could comprise **the potential product.**

_____

_____

_____

_____

Competitive product positioning

Key Management Concept

The factors that comprise the 'augmented product' are used by the marketer to position the total product competitively against the opposition in the marketplace. They don't just provide an advantage, they provide a competitive differential. This technique is known as competitive positioning, also as market positioning, product positioning and most frequently as just 'positioning'.

A product's position in a particular market is perceived in the mind of its prospects and/or customers. It is represented in the beliefs they have about how well the product satisfies their needs compared to how well competitor products do this. Positioning is crucially important since over time it measures the relative effectiveness of a company's strategy versus the competition. Often a product may occupy different positions in different markets. For example, Mercedes is perceived as a good taxi in Germany – but an up-market car in the UK.

Positioning strategies involve communicating to customers unique or superior offerings tailored to their needs. Positioning should reflect genuine attributes of the product and be matched to buyer preferences and characteristics. Customers cannot be fooled for long, if at all.

Thus in the car business:

- Porsche target 'wealthy sporty' users with its high performance.

- Volvo target the safety conscious with tough, crumple-zone safety features.

- Rolls-Royce target the 'wealthy' who want status with ultra-quality throughout.

Establishing positioning requires in-depth customer research to identify needs and prime buying criteria. Since positioning is also about beating rivals it requires research of competitor-offerings so as to know how to be superior. The company can then provide and promote a bundle of benefits more tightly fitted to customer needs than rival offerings.

Positioning maps

Positioning analysis often incorporates the use of one or more positioning maps. A hypothetical and simple two-variable example is shown in Figure 4.2 opposite.

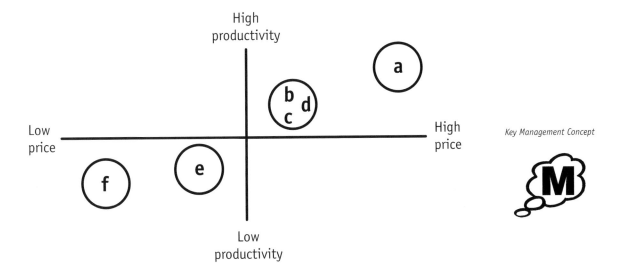

Key Management Concept

Figure 4.2: A hypothetical positioning map

- The horizontal and vertical axes show the prime customer supplier selection criteria as 'price' and 'productivity' respectively.

- The circled areas represent customer segments.

- A, B, C, D, E and F represent positions that are currently occupied by competitors.

- Analysis reveals the segment second up from the bottom (segment E) is not currently being served to the customer's satisfaction. Hence, there is an opportunity here for a company to enter this market by offering a product more closely positioned to customer needs than that being offered by rival E.

Analysis such as that in Figure 4.2 is useful. However, much greater clarity and completeness can be gained by using multi variate maps. These can illustrate the positions of several companys' products on all the factors that customers use as buying criteria. The hypothetical example of a PC market positioning shown in Figure 4.3 is, for simplicity, confined to eight buying criteria and just two companies. This type of positioning map is called a 'spidergram'.

Key Management Concept

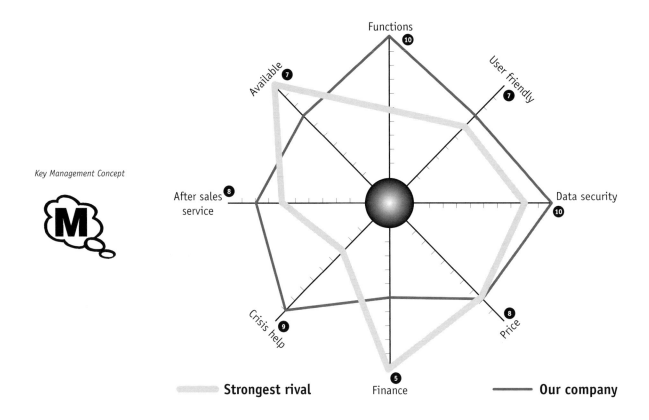

Figure 4.3: Hypothetical spidergram positioning map

In Figure 4.3 the eight axes of the spidergram radiate like bicycle wheel spokes from the hub in the centre. They relate to the customer's buying criteria and the number at the end of each spoke indicates the buying importance to the customers on a 10-point scale.

The lines joining the axes show the positioning of the two companies. They are defined by customers assessing each company's offering on a 10-point scale to express how well each offering satisfies the buying criteria. These scores are marked on the axes and the marks are jointed to form a continuous positioning line around the hub.

A further sophistication (*not shown*) is that instead of each of the axis being weighted as in the diagram, customer's buying criteria is itself expressed by (*in this case*) a third 'web' line. The use of different colours to indicate which web is which, assists clarity.

In this Figure, the unbroken positioning line refers to our company and the half tone line refers to our strongest rival. Thus, our company is superior on product functions, user friendliness, data security, crisis help and after sales service whereas the rival is superior on price, financing and availability.

These spidergram positionings indicate that our company has stronger appeal to benefits-orientated buyers while the rival is more attractive to price conscientious buyers. On balance, our company seems to have overall differential advantage since it is markedly superior on the three most important buying criteria (*functions, data security and crisis help*). Even so, both companies have scope to strengthen their positionings by improving their respective performance on the variables where they are inferior.

Positioning strategies

Key Management Concept

Various positioning options are available for companies entering a market:

- Position close to leader as 'acceptable alternative'
- Position away from existing rivals in either
  - unserved niches; or
  - innovative new positions.

For an existing market brand leader, sensible positionings include:

- Heavy promotion of existing superiority

- Augmenting present superiorities with extra layers of differential advantage (*see Levitt, page 114*).

For those badly positioned the options include:

- Adapting the offering to fit more closely with needs

- Finding new positionings

- Trying to alter customer perceptions (*but only if they are erroneous*)

- Withdrawing from the market.

Guidelines for effective positioning

Positioning is more effective when the 4Cs shown below are applied:

- **Clarity**. Target markets should be clearly defined and offerings tightly tailored to buyer needs.

- **Competitive**. The positioning must be based on superior buyer value or lower buyer costs (*You can't be both – it is not credible*).

- **Credibility**. The buyer benefit claimed by the company's promotion should be genuine, If not:

  a) no repeat sales and

  b) no customer recommendation.

- **Consistency**. A particular positioning will strengthen cumulatively the longer it is maintained. Efforts should therefore be made to select a positioning that is durable. Once established it should not be tinkered with, except if absolutely necessary.

Activity No. 6

Positioning your product

Construct a perceptual positioning map or spidergram for two products you know well, one yours, the other your strongest rival (*as per exercise Part 2, Chapter 2*).

Firstly

Decide on six factors used by your customers to evaluate your product.

Secondly

- Show them on the six axis form provided (*see over*).

- Grade each (out of ten) as to their importance to your customers (*again – it is wise to do your research rather than guess*).

- Join these grade points.

Thirdly

- Grade each axis as to how well you think your product addresses these issues versus the chosen competitor's product.

- Join the grade points for each product with a different coloured pen.

- Compare customers' needs versus your comparative offering, versus that of the competitor.

What does this reveal in terms of the key positioning issues your product faces?

Exercise – your positioning

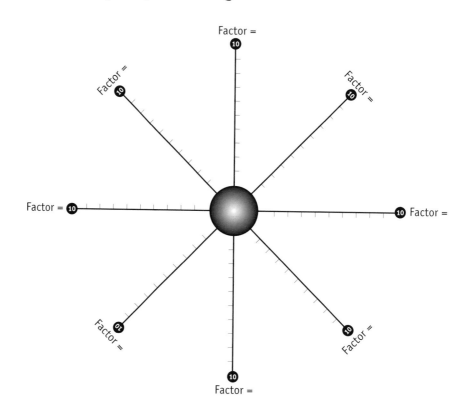

Colour:

Key:

[_____]   **Customer importance**

[_____]   **Competitors**

[_____]   **How you perform**

The marketing mix

Marketing pricing

Chapter 4: Part II

Introduction

Pricing is what marketing is all about. As we saw in Chapter 1, the whole point of the practice of marketing is to ensure the long-term survival of the company, and survival will only be assured if the company is profitable in the long-term. However, pricing is more than a score card, the better the company's marketing the higher the profit (*in the long-term at least*). Pricing is also a dynamic element of the marketing mix. Price can effect the way customers behave, and it will impact on their perceptions of value they may get from the company's offering.

This part of Chapter 4 examines market pricing in outline. We first review the conventional internal accounting based methods such as Cost-Plus, and its alter ego marginal pricing and their pitfalls. We then revisit the PLC and examine its impact on the marketer's freedom of manoeuvre re. pricing.

Via a short review of the principles behind 'value added pricing' we then conclude with a description of the most popular of the various marketing pricing strategies and their uses.

Internal accounting based pricing

Various studies have shown that the large majority of companies in British Industry (*circa 80%*) base their pricing policy on what is known as the Cost-Plus method. Its principles and shortcomings are reviewed below. From time to time these shortcomings have provoked companies to seek alternative methods, though still based on internal accounting. The most popular is marginal pricing – a method which still has shortcomings, one of which is a vicious trap for the unwary.

Cost-Plus

The Cost-Plus (*sometimes referred to as 'mark-up' pricing*) method of pricing is elegantly simple, easy to understand, easy to justify to customers, and very difficult for the marketer to argue with, particularly if they don't have the Figures. Accountants are rarely eager to share these with all and sundry in the company, whatever their ostensible reason, to do so is to part with their source of power in the company. However, the Cost-Plus method has fatal flaws, it can often make otherwise successful products appear to be unprofitable, it does not optimise revenue or margin in the long-term, and does not allow price to play its part in influencing customer behaviour favourably. Nor does it allow pricing to respond flexibly to the changes in market conditions brought about by such factors as the product life cycle, business cycle, or supply and demand. Therefore Cost-Plus is not an 'effectiveness' strategy.

The principles behind Cost-Plus are:

Key Management Concept

- take the cost of a product (*e.g. 100.00*)

- multiply this 'cost' by some ratio (*e.g. say a 50% 'mark-up'*)

- add the one to the other (*£100.00 + £50.00*) and that's the price before discount or tax. (*i.e. £150.00*).

The problem is two-fold:

i)   what is the true cost, and

ii) by what ratio should this be 'marked-up'?

Taking the last first:

Mark-up ratio

Frequently the ratio of 'mark-up' is based on 'tradition' – this industry has always done it this way e.g. a tailor prices the suit as the cost of the cloth times two, the same ratio is frequently used in market research. The dry-goods grocer marks-up by 10%, the greengrocer by 35%, architects by 12.5% etc., but why? It has always been done this way.

Some businesses, such as trainers and consultants, arrive at their price by a slightly more tortuous route:

- take the total overhead (*rent, rates, car lease etc. say all comes to £25,000 pa.*)

- add the desired income for the year ahead (*say £60,000 pa*)

- now divide this total figure by the number of working days in the year (*200 days not counting weekends, but less say 20 days for holidays, 50 days for administration, 30 days for selling etc. = 100 days left for working*)

- this equates to £85,000 revenue required from 100 days work = £850.00 per day. But the going rate for trainers is £1,200 per day and if that person quotes £850.00 per day they will be saying to many customers, not that they are more of a bargain, but that they are **not** as good as the mainstream.

The true cost

Key Question

For all but the one-product company, this is a nightmare. What share of the company's central overhead (*e.g. head office, training, human resources, legal team, research and development etc.*) should different items in the product range carry?

The most important thing to appreciate is that it is inordinately difficult to decide what is the actual cost of a product or service. For a multi service/product company the so called 'fixed costs' per product, or transaction, or relationship can be no more than an opinion based on that particular company's 'attribution' policies. (*Just as price is a policy, based on an opinion of the effect it will have on the attainment of the company's market/business objectives*).

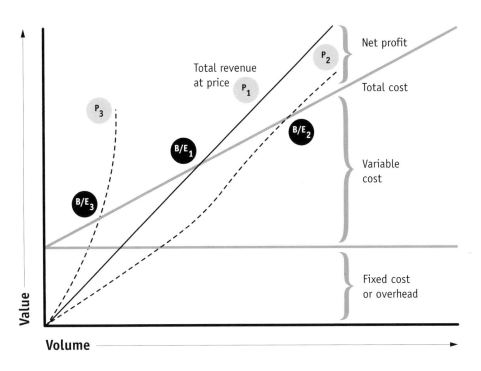

Figure 4.4: Simple break-even

If we consider Figure 4.4, it looks so reasonable. At price one, we break-even, at point one. Were we to charge a slightly lower price, we would break-even later, and if a slightly higher price, we would break-even earlier. But the problem is that the characteristics of modern products, particularly when value is added via services, (*i.e. their intangibility, inseparability, heterogeneity, etc.*) all make it very difficult, perhaps in some cases, even impossible, to calculate the real costs of providing any one product or service episode.

Consider the following two examples:

Spreading the unspreadable (i)
[O/H = admin ÷ labour @ % = 150%]

£000

Product	A	B	C	Total
Sales	170	320	670	1,160
Materials	90	30	150	270
Labour	10	130	100	240
Other direct costs	20	40	150	210
Totals (prime)	120	200	400	720
Contributions	50	120	270	440
Central overheads*	15	195	150	360
Profit /(loss)	35	(75)	120	80

Figure 4.5

Spreading the unspreadable (ii)
[O/H = admin ÷ prime = 50%]

£000

Product	A	B	C	Total
Sales	170	320	670	1,160
Materials	90	30	150	270
Labour	10	130	100	240
Other direct costs	20	40	150	210
Totals (prime)	120	200	400	720
Contributions	50	120	270	440
Central overheads*	60	100	200	360
Profit /(loss)	(10)	20	70	80

Figure 4.6

In Figure 4.5 the apportionment of overhead is allocated as per the ratio of total administration divided by the cost of labour, which in this example is 150% (*as a percentage of the cost of the labour that has gone into the product*). The bottom line is that whilst the service product 'A' makes £35,000 and the service product 'C' is handsomely profitable, the service product 'B' appears to be losing money.

However, if we examine another way of breaking the overhead, in example Figure 4.6, here the ratio is of the total administration divided by the prime cost, and this works out at a ratio of 50% (*of the prime cost of the item*). Under these circumstances, product 'A' is now making a loss, whilst product 'B' is marginally profitable and product 'C' is reasonably profitable, but nowhere near as profitable as it was before. The dilemma, quite simply, is which of these situations is right, if any?

One thing is absolutely certain, if we are prompted by the first example to drop product 'B' (because apparently it is unprofitable), the overhead carried by product 'B' (£195,000) will have to be spread between product 'A' and product 'C', the contribution being made by product B will of course come off the bottom line, and the total business will be making a **loss** of some £40,000.

Key Management Concept

In the second situation, if we were to drop product 'A', (*which now looks unprofitable*), the overhead carried by 'A' will similarly have to be spread over 'B' and 'C' and the contribution from 'A' would be lost. The contribution being £50,000 would reduce our total profitability down to £30,000.

Of these two examples, the better case is the second choice. At least we still make a relatively small profit, whereas in the first choice, we will be making a hefty loss by the deletion of product 'B'.

The history of business is rife with such examples of catastrophic decisions being taken as the result of misleading overhead allocation. At one time, a major UK bank nearly tore itself apart because of the way its overhead costs, particularly those from branches which were allocated across the organisation. The accountants at the top of the organisation were ex-branch people and the regime that they had established was to allocate overhead according to the ratio of turnover of that part of the business, i.e. by branch. So the more turnover a particular part of the business did, the more of the overhead it actually carried.

But corporate banking, whose main business was to provide cash transfer for client organisations, required no branch network, had an extremely high turnover and therefore carried a disproportionately unfair amount of the bank's overhead. Eventually the extent of this attribution made corporate banking uncompetitive in the marketplace.

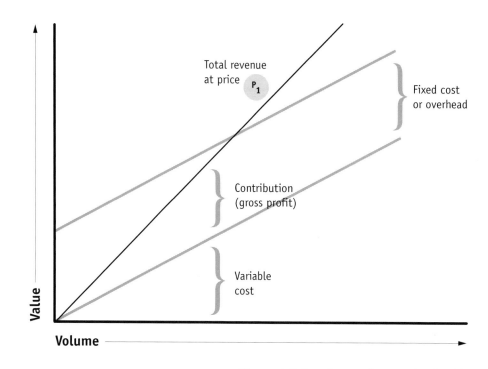

Figure 4.7: Break-even for marginal pricing

Marginal pricing

Faced with the dilemma posed by 'Cost-Plus', many organisations have opted for what is known as a 'marginal pricing' approach.

For this approach, as we can see in Figure 4.7 (opposite), variable cost is placed on the bottom axis and the fixed cost or overhead is drawn as the space between the line drawn parallel to the variable cost line. 'Contribution' is that amount in excess of variable cost (i.e. the margin) that the organisation is able to charge its customers. The hope is that by the end of the financial year, all the contributions from the various jobs and projects add up to more than the total overhead of the company. This may be the case when times are good. The temptation is, however, that when times are hard, in order to be competitive, the business will price its work so as to make only a small contribution above variable cost. Under these circumstances, it can easily be the case that by the end of the financial year all these contributions **do not** add up to the total overhead. Eventually the company runs out of capital and goes bust, which is the main problem with a marginal pricing strategy.

Key Management Concept

The overhead ratio and price

There is one area in business where a knowledge of variable costs verses fixed costs is vital when deciding pricing policy. When the ratio of overhead to variable cost is high, the marketer must adopt a pricing policy that alters the prices charged as the product moves towards break-even. To fail to break-even in a situation like this would be extremely dangerous for the company, because the high overhead provides a particularly un-forgiving burden.

If however, the ratio of overhead to variable cost is low then paradoxically, there is far greater room for manoeuvre, and failure to break-even is not so severely punished.

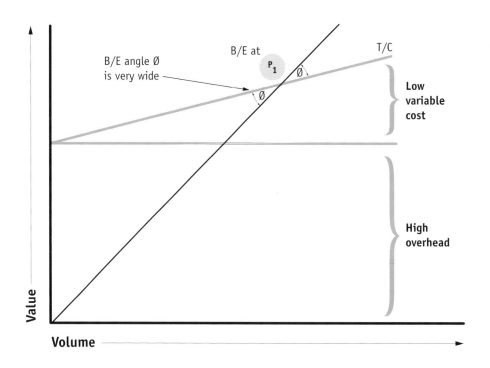

Figure 4.8: Where the ratio of overhead to variable cost is high

Key Learning Point

As can be seen in Figure 4.8, the angle theta at Ø, at which price P breaks-even, is very wide. This means that a small increment either above or below break-even has a disproportionate effect on profitability. A good example of this is an airline. For an airline route such as crossing the Atlantic, the cost of flying one extra passenger before or after break-even, is a relatively small amount of fuel. All the other elements of cost are relatively fixed. No extra meals are required, no extra staff, no extra administration, and so forth. However, the extra revenue represented by one passenger at or before break-even, is quite considerable, particularly if they are a business class passenger. So that flight will be at least a thousand pounds below break-even if one such passenger doesn't turn up, or will enjoy a thousand pounds above break-even if one extra passenger does turn up. For every passenger that the plane is below break-even, a considerable cost is incurred. The losses from a flight that falls short will have to be made up from flights that don't fall short. Therefore the strategy in such a case must be to go for volume and adopt pricing strategies which are designed specifically to achieve that end.

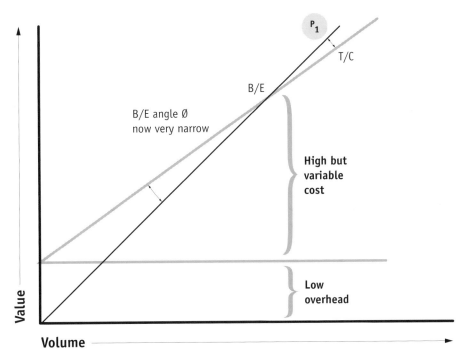

Figure 4.9: Where the ratio of overhead to variable cost is low

However, consider Figure 4.9, here we see a situation where the overhead is kept particularly low as a ratio of variable cost. In the circumstance the amount by which a company is going to suffer by falling short of break-even, (*or profit if it exceeds break-even*) is relatively small. Under these circumstances the company's policies must be designed to pursue value.

So for a high ratio the rule of thumb is, volume dominates, and for a low ratio, value dominates.

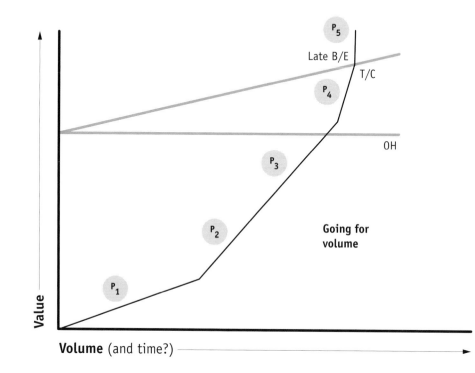

Figure 4.10: Pricing strategy for high overheads/ variable cost ratios (e.g. for airliners and trainers)

The approach to pricing that a business with a high fixed to variable cost ratio must adopt is shown in Figure 4.10. Two types of business exemplify this approach: an airline and a trainer in business.

In both circumstances, the bottom axis not only represents the volume of business but also time. In exactly the same way that a product manager for an airline route will have a year before the flight to try to load every seat in the plane, so a business trainer will have about a year's worth of diary being booked ahead at any one time. In both cases the ultimate strategy is to sell the initial business relatively cheap so as to go for volume and cover the overhead. Therefore anyone buying business at that time, from such an organisation, should be able to obtain quite a considerable bargain.

Key Management Concept

In the case of airlines, this early part of the business is exemplified by some form of PEX tickets, like APEX and so forth. An APEX ticket is non-refundable, so if the passenger does not fly, they don't get their money back. Thus for, let's say, the first four or five months of any particular flight's booking life, prices for the back of the plane are very reasonable. The closer we get towards break-even and the closer we get to the time when the plan must fly, then the steeper the prices will become, such that in the weeks and days immediately before the plane's flight is due, there are hardly any discounts available and certainly no special deals. The reasoning being that anyone who books a particular flight so close to the date must need to travel on that flight and therefore will be relatively less price sensitive than one who has booked twelve months ahead.

At break-even the situation will change dramatically. At that point the trainer and the airline product manager both know that they will cover their costs. Any extra business, particularly that booked at short notice, should therefore be charged at a premium. This is particularly true for business trainers because there is a real opportunity cost of their time. At this point it will be a scarce commodity in exactly the same way as there will be relatively few seats left on the plane. So, both organisations, working with supply and demand on their side, can charge a premium price. The trainer has to do this in order to ration time which would otherwise be available for curriculum development, writing books etc. The airline has to do this so as to compensate for the losses made on flights that don't reach break-even. So the airline product manager will usually give instructions at this point to those preparing the plane for flight to maximise, if possible, the business class and first class areas of the plane.

Implications of overheads/variable cost ratios on resource capacity strategies

Key Management Concept

The maintenance of the quality of service delivery is most easily accomplished by maintaining sufficient resource capacity in-house. However, a few moments thought about this overheads/variable cost (OH/VC) ratio will explain why so many organisations are being tempted to become 'virtual companys'. The cost advantages of not owning (*or even leasing*) your own planes, computers, bookings facilities, cabin crew, maintenance facilities and so forth are tempting.

The ownership of all this resource will incur a large overhead, whereas if the service company could use subcontractors as and when required, these costs become **variable** and the pressures on price to go for volume, rather than value, evaporate.

In the case of an airline, this can represent a tremendous extra profitability per seat. In addition, airlines (*and any other similar business*) would have much lower break-even points with less sleepless nights for the financial director.

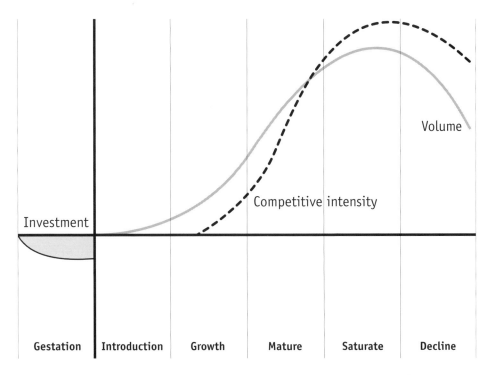

Figure 4.11: Product life cycle showing investment and competition

Product life cycle and price

If 'supply and demand' (*ref: Chapter 1 'The power of marketing'*) is the prime consideration then the PLC is the second major issue in terms of market forces that affect price, Chapter 1 has provided a brief overview of the PLC. This concept is important because its different stages each have an optimum pricing strategy.

Figure 4.11 details two issues that the marketer must bear in mind when setting prices. The first one is the amount of investment that occurs during the gestation period, i.e. that point at which the product and/or its technology are being developed. A considerable amount of investment is made up to the point of launch, and this investment must be recouped. However, there are forces in the marketplace that militate against this. The most important of which is of course the severity of competition.

As we can see in Figure 4.11 as a new product demonstrates that a market exists (*by moving out of the introduction phase into the growth phase*) competitors are attracted to the market. It will be seen that the maturity phase of the life cycle is characterised by growing and intense competition. Competitive intensity peaks slightly later than the saturation period, at this point the fight gets more desperate. The reason for this is that during the maturity phase, everyone's business is growing and any increase in market share is usually not perceived by the competitors as being business taken from them. During saturation the market is effectively stagnant, any loss of market share is felt immediately and the reaction from those companies losing their market share is often aggressive. The marketer launching a new product must therefore anticipate this with their pricing strategy. As we can see in Figure 4.12 (opposite), the ultimate strategy is to start high at the launch, and gradually bring price down over time to counter the rise in competitive intensity as it occurs.

Key Learning Point

Not all new products are successful, in some markets it can be as low as only one success in fourteen launches, so the marketer must be concerned to ensure that when products do succeed, the company recoups their development and launch costs early on. They will not have the opportunity to do so later, because competitive aggressiveness increases over time.

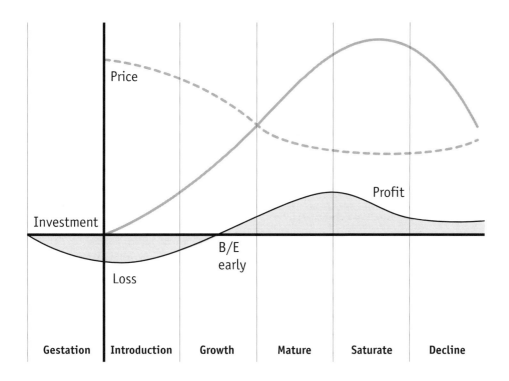

Figure 4.12: Product life cycle showing a 'skimming' price and effect on profit

This pricing strategy is called 'skimming', it starts high to take the cream from the top of the market and then reduces over time to combat competition. The affect on profit is quite dramatic as will be seen. Under these conditions the marketer cannot expect to recoup the total development costs until probably well into the growth phase. The total profit of the operation will probably peak sometime during the middle of the maturity phase. As undesirable as 'skimming' may initially appear, it is probably the only option for many marketers in markets undergoing dynamic innovation, such as IT.

However, there are some marketers who, by employing a supporting marketing mix, are able to use price as a means of keeping the competition out of (*or at least severely constrained within*) their marketplace. This we can see happening in Figure 4.13 below.

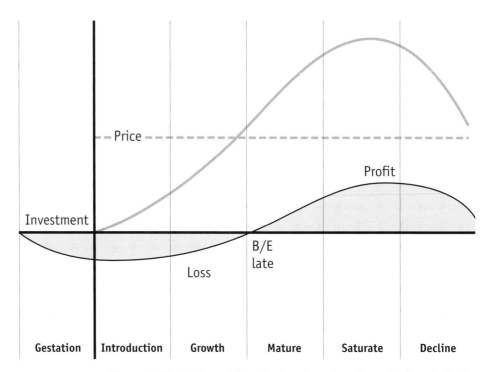

Figure 4.13: Product life cycle showing the effect of a 'barrier' price

A barrier price is where a marketer has the courage to start their pricing low, thus making the marketplace unattractive for competition, at least in the very early stages of the life cycle. The aim is to make it unattractive throughout the whole life cycle.

As would be expected, it takes longer to recoup the initial development and launch costs. However, profitability is sustained throughout the maturity and saturation stages of the life cycle and maybe well into decline. The foremost proponent of this strategy is a major international glass company who have world wide patents on their technology to produce 'float glass'. In many countries they also own the main sources of silica sand for the glass making process. These elements, together with strong and comprehensive distribution and promotion, combine to make their market very unattractive for outside players. By the time a competitor has paid a licence fee for the right to use the patented process, and perhaps even bought the silica sand from the glass company itself, the margins (*if there are any*) are so slim that the new entrant could get better return on their investment elsewhere.

It is very rare for a marketer to have such control over the whole mix and so, if in doubt, a skimming pricing strategy is the option of choice.

Value added pricing

The principle behind 'value added' pricing is that price is tied to the customer's perception of what the product is worth to them. To do this the marketer has to be able to put a value on the 'augmented' aspects of the product and also on aspects of the 'potential' which may be brought into play in response to market conditions. (*see the 'Levitt Construct', page 114*)

Thus the marketer must understand how their customers perceive quality and value in what they are offered. The process is firstly to identify:

- Who is involved (*i.e. which members of the decision making unit*)?

- Whereabouts is the product in its life cycle?

- How might this vary with members of the decision making unit?

- To what extent can people influence the feelings of value within the client business?

For each of the foregoing types of people and circumstances, the marketer identifies the key objective and subjective factors that are involved, what priority these factors have and how the product in question stacks up against the competition in the minds of those involved. Does it offer superior value, does it offer opportunities to the service marketer, what are the negatives, and what are the problems?

$$\text{Value perceived (Vp)} = \frac{\text{Perceived benefits}}{\text{Perceived costs}}$$

Where $Vp \geqslant 1$ Customer delighted

Where $Vp < 1$ Customer disappointed

Where $Vp > 1.25$ or more   Customer is suspicious

Figure 4.14: Perception of value

As we see in Figure. 4.14, a customer's perception of value is a function of perceived relative benefits divided by perceived relative costs. Such that where perceived value is equal to or greater than unity, the customer is delighted, where perceived value is less than this, the customer is disappointed. Also, where the perceived value is too good to be true, (*in this instance greater than 1.25*), customers become suspicious.

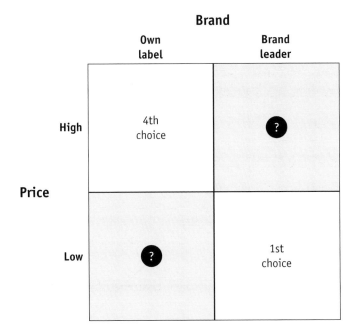

Figure 4.15: The principle of conjoint (trade-off) analysis

As a concept this sounds all very well and good, but how do you actually measure the customer's expectations and perceptions of cost versus their perceptions of relative benefits? Here a market research tool, referred to either as a 'conjoint analysis' or a 'trade-off analysis' steps into the breach.

Like all good ideas the principles of conjoint analysis are quite simple to understand. The practice, however, can be very complex particularly as many variables are employed in this mathematical modelling technique.

Consider Figure 4.15, where we have a 2 x 2 matrix, the horizontal axis being the brand, and the vertical axis being price. Branding is divided into own label on the left and the brand leader, in that field, on the right. Price is divided into high for the top, and low for the bottom.

Consider a customer being asked to choose in what order they would purchase on this matrix. The first part is a sanity check. The first choice of all but the abnormal would be the brand leader at the lowest possible price. The own label at the highest price would be their last choice, (*if they don't do this they can be discounted from the sample as being outside the target group*). Which of those remaining choices now taking second and third place, will tell us a great deal about how customers make a trade-off between brand and price?

Conjoint analysis takes this principle and applies it to situations where there are more than just one set of brand choices. There will also be a wider range of choice in price than just high or low. Additionally it will also examine other trade offs that might be presented to the customer, such as colour, time factors, availability, speed of reaction, and so forth; together with other ancillary factors that may be used to add value to the 'augmented' part of the product. Mathematical reasoning then puts a utility value on each of the factors investigated and builds a model which enables a service marketer to be able to answer 'what if' questions.

(*A good source paper for the reader is 'Axelrod & Frendburg', 'Conjoint Analysis: Peering Behind the Jargon', J.O.M. 1987*).

Price as an indicator of quality

Under the right conditions price can often be a major indicator of the quality of the products for sale. Nowhere is this more true than where service is used to add value. The basic conditions for this situation exist in services because the product is not only intangible and therefore prone to a great deal of subjective appraisal, but in addition it cannot be sampled. Thus, prior to purchase, much of the offering is a promise which can only be evaluated **after** commitment.

The basic conditions that must exist for customers to use price as an indicator of quality are if one or more of the following apply:

- There is little or no product information available to the customer. In other words the customer is essentially naive about the product and is unable to make an informed judgment. If the purchase is important enough, it is also important to make sure that they get it right. Therefore, customers will use price to inform their behaviour.

- There may be no other evaluative criteria available, or there are perceived to be major quality differences between brands. The issue is the word 'perceived'. The marketer's battle ground is in the mind of the customer and it is their perceptions, as we have seen elsewhere, that govern their behaviour.

- If the cost consequences of making bad decisions are great, and/or if the product has a high level of socio-economic significance. In both these situations the customer is apt to perceive a high level of risk.

- The buyers and/or other important members of the decision making unit have confidence that price in their marketplace, is an indicator of quality.

Consultancy services are located towards the intellectual property end of the service spectrum and are considered to have a high requirement for credibility. In these areas price also remains an important factor as an indicator of quality **after** consumption. The greater the perceived risk and cost of a product going wrong, the greater chance that a price reduction can damage the image of the product.

Any marketer should give a great deal of thought when contemplating price reductions. They could also detrimentally affect the image of the product via hurting the egos of those who have already purchased.

If service is of relatively short duration, (*i.e. it doesn't take a long time to deliver*) but it yields benefits over a much longer period, for example in terms of training or consultancy, the marketer, as a means of supporting price, must include strategies to drive home the long-term investment nature of the product.

Some useful marketing pricing strategies

Key Learning Point

Finally lets look at the classic marketing pricing strategies together with brief explanations as to their workings and benefits.

Penetration pricing

A low price which helps the marketer get into the new marketplace.

Premium pricing

A high price designed to reinforce strategies that put the product at the top of its marketplace. Specifically used in markets where price is seen as an indicator of quality, such as in the early days of mobile phones for example.

Price skimming

This strategy starts off as premium price, but is deliberately designed to come down over time to anticipate or react to competitive or other pressures in the market. As its name implies, it takes the cream from the top of the market, it can also be used as a means of 'shepherding' demand and thereby relieving the pressures on resource capacity.

Promotional pricing

Special price deals that are designed to support all other marketing activity that may be involved in a particular promotion, such as, advertising, public relations, special deals at distributors and so forth.

Line pricing

This is designed to reflect the position of a product in the range on offer from that supplier, so that at the top of the range, the prices would be premium, at the bottom of the range they would be the lowest possible. Products between these two extremes would be priced pro rata.

Bait pricing

Pricing strategy is that which is designed to make it relatively cheap for a customer to enter the market by offering a very low price for the very basic and standard version of the product. The customer is then free to (*indeed, may be encouraged to*) add extras, at an increased price of course, from a menu of optional extras. A good example of this would be a chain of hotels designed specifically for the business community. The quoted price for a room would give the occupant a basic level of accommodation, but no more. If guests wished to watch the television, that's extra; if they wished to have breakfast in the hotel, again that's extra.

Dual or multiple pricing

This is where the same product is sold in several different markets. The 'core' and the 'expected' parts, and maybe even for a substantial proportion of the 'augmented', are identical. But these products are marketed to **different segments** and each segment has its own price, which will differ from any other segment, some higher, some lower.

This strategy can only be successful if it is difficult, if not impossible, for a set of customers in one segment to communicate and/or compare their product offering with customers in a different segment. Hampering inter-customer communications can be brought about by ensuring that one set of customers cannot even meet up with any other segments, or if they do, it is very difficult for them to compare the offering in their segment with the offerings in others.

A good example of this is the segmentation policy that airlines employ. All passengers are accommodated within the same aluminium tube when flying from one airport to another, hopefully they all take off and land at the same time. However, the airline marketer has made it possible to charge substantially more for those people who sit in the front of the aircraft compared to those people who sit in the back. They can do this because business class and first class are usually provided with substantial augmentation to the product, i.e. VIP lounges at airports, wider seats, free drinks, more space etc. All with a lower probability of being 'bounced' (*i.e. moved to a later flight*).

Finally a marketer can use dual pricing when he/she develops a 'fighter brand'. A 'fighter brand' is a product launched specifically to do damage to a competitor via the use of low, sometimes even predatory prices. When the objective is accomplished and the competitor either withdraws or is reduced to bankruptcy, a marketer will kill off the fighter brand and resume business with the main product that stayed aloof during the price war and whose image is thus not contaminated with a lower price. It is often a lot easier to put prices down than it is to restore them afterwards.

Predatory pricing

This is a policy designed to put competitors out of the marketplace. In some countries this is illegal, but not (*on the whole*) in the United Kingdom.

A good example of the employment of predatory pricing was the battle in 1996 between *The Times* and *The Daily Telegraph* (*on the one side*) and *The Independent* (*on the other*). *The Times* and *The Daily Telegraph* aimed aggressive predatory pricing strategies against *The Independent* in the hope of driving it out of the market.

However, after some dramatic reorganisation, the Board of *The Independent* were able to link up with a syndicate of other European newspapers for support and thus increased the size of its war chest. When faced with the prospect of a long and costly war of attrition, *The Times* and *The Daily Telegraph* ceased their pricing policy.

It is interesting to note that this episode served to increase the overall circulation of all broadsheet newspapers in the United Kingdom, whilst at the same time, proving a salutary experience to *The Independent* who, by the fall of 1997, had repositioned their paper out of the segment that put them head to head with *The Times* and *The Daily Telegraph*, and into the segment occupied by *The Guardian*, one of the only national broadsheet newspapers (the other being *The Financial Times*) that had not been adversely affected by the former predatory pricing war.

Barrier pricing

As we have seen when we examined the effect of the product life cycle on pricing strategy, this is a pricing policy that, by being potentially very unprofitable, is designed to make the marketplace unattractive for competitors.

Partnership or relationship pricing

This is a strategy we will look at in more detail in a moment, but essentially partnership pricing is designed to foster long-term business between two or more organisations. Although it is not the 'be-all-and-end-all' of the Japanese Kiretsu system, it is something which is at the heart of it.

Price as a shepherd

The marketer may be required to relieve pressure on resources, or to channel customers into one segment rather than another. For example, for business travel services, a premium price can be used at peak times and a highly discounted price for other times of the day/week/year.

In those services, where a great deal of social interaction takes place, varying the price of a service can vary the types of people that use it. In those services which are characterised by having high levels of inter-customer contact and involvement (*and/or where customers use other customers as an indicator of the quality of the service that they are contemplating*), to mix the wrong sorts of people on any one occasion in any one service, can have a very negative effect on the perception of its quality.

So the service marketer will use price to move one set of people to the 'up-market' end of the product range, whilst deterring, via the use of price, those who would not be accepted in this segment. A good example of this being the segregation of those attending a horse racecourse where the 'Silver Ring' enclosure is cheaper than the 'Members' enclosure, and a lot less 'select'.

Relationship/partnership pricing

The intention of this pricing strategy is to build long-term relationships. The strategy itself comprises several objectives, one being to raise the barriers to entry for competitors and the other, ironically, is to raise the hurdle of pain that would have to be overcome by customers who may be contemplating placing their business elsewhere.

The relationship/partnership pricing strategy consists of four main parts:

- Firstly, a 'service level agreement' between the two (or more) parties. This would set out agreed delivery times, speeds of response, levels of availability, cleanliness of vehicles, frequency of meetings etc.

- Secondly, it would include open book accounting between the parties involved, so that the service provider can charge all agreed and certifiable costs as incurred.

- Thirdly, there would usually be a management fee (*frequently negotiated on an annual basis*), which is sometimes negotiated as an agreed ratio of overall expenditure, as for example, in several large and famous advertising agencies, or a fixed monetary amount as perhaps might be the case for a company providing hauler services.

- Lastly, there would be a performance bonus, this again would be negotiated, also perhaps on an annual or some other periodic basis. The bonus being tied directly to the suppliers performance against the service level agreement as above.

   The principle behind the following structure is that:

   – with the cost and management fee, the service provider can only break-even

   – to make any profit at all, they will have to perform up to and beyond the service level agreed to earn the bonuses negotiated.

The instance of relationship pricing is on the increase, particularly amongst those companies providing business to business services for which the customer would have a constant requirement. A particularly good example of a relationship pricing strategy is cited in the BBC video of the Tom Peter's presentation 'Management Imagination': the case of Lanes Transport of Bristol and their pricing arrangements with the Body Shop organisation.

Profit centre

Add to all the foregoing the question as to what is the actual profit centre of a business that has a wide range of products and activities. Should it be the branches for example, where the service is actually delivered? Should it be the transaction itself, like cashing a cheque, or using a credit card? Or perhaps it should be the product, like insurance or breakfast cereal, or yet again, perhaps the centre of profit should be the total customer relationship.

All of these options for pricing strategy should be carefully considered in the light of the company's marketing objectives, so as to discover which is the most appropriate.

The marketing mix

Your route to market – distribution

Chapter 4: Part III

Introduction

No matter how good the rest of the mix, if the customer can't find a place to buy it from – either a company who stocks it, or who can order it for them – then all the effort so far is wasted, nothing will be sold.

However, unlike the other three elements of the marketing mix, distribution decisions often involve the 'management' of external companies, i.e. they require *inter*-organisation in addition to *intra*-organisational skills.

Distribution channel decisions also tend to be far more inflexible than the other mix elements, particularly where intermediaries are involved.

Background

The 'route to market' element of the marketing mix, is divided into two main components:

Key Management Concept

1. *A distribution channel*, i.e. a set of other companies which help move the product from its point of production to its point of sale.

2. *Channel management*, i.e. the management processes which handles the relationships between channel members.

The three dimensions of the distribution decision are:

1. Environmental

2. Structural

3. Behavioural

The environmental dimension

The starting point for understanding the nature of distribution should be the environmental dimension. The tools, techniques and frameworks introduced in the macro analysis are essential to identify key trends (*i.e. the P.L.E.E.S.T [political, legal, economic, environmental, social and technological] analysis, Chapter 6*).

Key Learning Point

For example, developments in digital technology have accelerated the convergence of the computer and telecommunications industries and in doing so transformed the market structure of the financial services industry. Traditional agency-based distribution channels can now be readily by-passed either by sophisticated database marketing systems, or increasingly, via the Internet.

Internationally, the political will to deregulate market structures also offers tremendous opportunities for global companies, particularly in countries such as Japan which have traditionally had long distribution channels.

Techniques for analysing the micro environment (*i.e. 'Porter's five forces', Chapter 6, page 275*) should also be employed to understand the company's competitive position before taking distribution channel decisions.

The structural dimension

The smaller company may well have this decision made for them – as we will see later – the freedom to choose how you get to market is a function of power. The larger the company, the more alternatives are available – the smaller the company, the greater the chance that the products will reach the market via the distributors who choose you.

If you are too small, or too new, or too innovative there may be no alternative but to go direct. Some great companies got started this way – Mars sold its morning's production that same afternoon in Slough market. RCA Records started by touting the 78s door to door by barrow. Today it's a lot easier via the Internet (*but that's a different book*).

Deciding on the 'structure' of the required routes to market will involve the marketer addressing several questions.

Firstly

Should intermediaries (*i.e. middlemen*) be used at all? This decision ultimately depends on a combination of what the customer needs and what the company has the resources and skills to do, and if an *indirect* approach is chosen.

Secondly

How many *levels* of distribution should be employed?

A *long* channel typically has a combination of national and regional distributors before *retailers* or *industrial intermediaries* provide the interface with the end-user.

A *short* channel is characterised by manufacturers dealing with large national retailers (e.g. Tescos, PC World, Carphone Warehouse) or national industrial dealers (e.g. RSC Components).

Thirdly

What is the level of specialism required from the dealer?

When the product in question is technologically simple and relatively 'self-contained', a *generalist* intermediary is common. Here the distributor is typically providing convenience and 'one-stop-shopping' for the end-user.

This is typical of mature markets, i.e. by this stage customers can specify almost exactly what they want so need no hand-holding.

However, when a product is technologically complex and/or is targeted at tightly defined niche markets then *specialist* distributors are required. Here the distributor often adds some value to the manufacturer's product via customising it in some way to meet the specific needs of the end-user. Such intermediaries form part of distribution systems often described as either *Value Added Re-sellers* (VARs) or *Value Added Dealer Networks* (VADNs).

Finally

What level of distribution intensity is required?

Exclusive intermediaries typically deal with a narrow product range and/or only handle the products of one manufacturer.

Intensive distribution channels give widespread market coverage to manufacturers whose customer base is widely dispersed.

Selective distribution lies somewhere between the two.

Often, the more exclusive the distribution channel, the more specialist the intermediary has to be.

Functions of the 'route to market'

There are three golden rules of distribution channel structure. The essence of which reflects the need for a number of functions when taking products from their *point of manufacture to their point of purchase*. These rules are:

Key Management Concept

i)   elements of any channel can be eliminated or substituted,

ii) however, their functions cannot be eliminated.

If i) then the relevant functions are moved forward or backward in the chain to be exercised by others.

In summary

A producer **can** by-pass distribution intermediaries but he/she **cannot** eliminate the functions which these organisations perform.

There are three basic functions of a 'route to market' (channel), they are:

1. Transactional

2. Logistical

3. Facilitating

Transactional functions cover a range of activities which collectively deliver widespread, lower cost market coverage. This category also embraces the primary activities of adding value via providing a *marketing* and sales function to the next link, and, with its emphasis on contacts with customers, it establishes market linkages via its buyer-seller relationships.

Logistical functions embrace a range of tasks associated with the physical distribution and handling of goods. The first three are, *assorting*, *storing* and *sorting*, i.e. they bulk-up the small orders of their customers, they break down the bulk delivery from their suppliers and they provide 'from stock' availability close to the market, and by so doing they deliver to the end customer the benefits of *one-stop-shopping*, availability and *choice*.

Facilitating functions sometimes referred to as 'logistics', ensure that goods *flow* through the channel smoothly.

Adding value is still part of the role, both pre- and post-purchase (e.g. packaging, servicing etc.) The *financing* of the inventory which flows through the channel can be a key facilitative function in some markets (e.g. construction).

This can range from:

- carrying the costs of holding the inventory – i.e. they tie-up **their** money in stock, not yours, to

- helping to finance the customers' purchase by providing access to capital, e.g. Estate Agents helping the buyer raise a mortgage; car dealers providing hire-purchase schemes; or even extending long lines of credit as per builders' merchants or agricultural suppliers such as seed merchants etc. This is to say they help the customer to buy if they don't have the cash.

Key Learning Point

These three fundamental distribution tasks can ensure the required level of availability and financing of cash flow and end-user convenience etc.

There are five important and discrete 'currents' in any 'route to market', they are:

Action Checklist

1. Products
2. Ownership
3. Payment
4. Promotion
5. Information

Some currents flow in only one direction, for example, products flow forward (toward the end customer) through the channel, payment flows (up the 'food chain') *backwards*.

Some transfers flow in both directions, for example, information. Typically, the greater the number of levels in the channel (or 'limits in the chain') the more complex becomes the pattern of these currents.

Fundamentally, channel structure relates to the number and complexity of functions which must be performed in taking the product from point of production to point of purchase. In some markets it must also address whatever post-purchase servicing may be required (e.g. *installation, maintenance, training etc.*) The key question is:

Key Question

Who in the supply chain is more likely to have the abilities to undertake these functions most effectively and efficiently, and is free and willing to do so?

The marketer must thus undertake a *distribution channel audit* to identify which functions need performing, and to evaluate who should undertake them – the manufacturer or an intermediary – and if the latter, who and what function will they be required to perform?

The principle of *specialisation and division of labour* tends to hold good. In today's complex world specialist tasks are probably best left to specialist organisations.

Using intermediaries: advantages and disadvantages

Many of the principal *advantages* of using distributors are derived from the core economics of supply chain management, for example, *market coverage, specialisation, customer contacts* and *lower costs*.

Other advantages relate to processes which facilitate the creation and implementation of effective marketing strategies, for example, *marketing knowledge, market segmentation* and *selling skills*.

Others link into value adding activities and logistical support, for example, *effective delivery, customer service (pre and post purchase), manufacturer services etc.*

Key Management Concept

The first *disadvantage* of using distributors emanates from perhaps the most fundamental issue in organisational behaviour, which is that typically organisations do not like ceding *control* to others i.e. external entities. They fear opportunistic behaviour and the possibility that intermediaries will *extract* rather than *add* value.

The second point is the *middleman's profit*. Producers often wrongly view intermediaries as *channel parasites* rather than *marketing assets*. This negative outlook underpins many of the additional *perceived* disadvantages such as:

- loss of control
- loss of customer contact
- loss of customer ownership etc.

The last two issues, 'contact' and 'ownership' can often inhibit the marketer's ability to apply the full range of marketing skills. If you don't own the customer – you will frequently be unable to contact them directly so as to get their views

– which means that market research will be more difficult and more expensive than it should be.

A possible way to circumvent this, if appropriate, is the use of customer's registration certificates, guarantee return certificates etc. However, this is a function of the marketer's power vs that of the intermediary.

The fear of *poor market management, inadequate communication* and that an *intermediary's objectives* may conflict with those of the producer can derive from poor past experiences of using distributors. However, this view of the situation undermines and negates the potential of a more open and constructive role for intermediaries.

Whatever the arguments for or against intermediaries, when used effectively, the middleman can add tremendous value and thus, should be *selected* and *managed* in a way that maximises their contribution via exploiting their *specialist* skills and facilities.

If the distribution channel audit reveals that intermediaries must be used, it makes sense to employ good *management* principles to create a constructive, positive relationship with the organisations in your route to market. This, in turn, will require an understanding of the *behavioural* dimensions of distribution channel management.

'Managing' the distribution channel

Push versus pull strategies

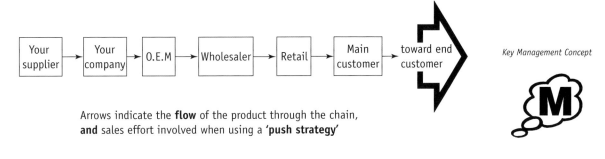

Arrows indicate the **flow** of the product through the chain,
and sales effort involved when using a **'push strategy'**

Figure 4.16: A channel 'push' strategy

Conventionally, and the way most intermediaries would prefer it, each company in the chain sells to the next one down the chain (Figure 4.16). This means that each link can play upstream suppliers one off against each other (as we saw in Chapter 1, Part II).

This behaviour, as shown above, is known as channel 'push' as each producer and every subsequent link in the chain tries to 'push' its products down through the pipeline. However, powerful and rich players can avoid being played off against their competitors via the adoption of a 'pull' strategy, as shown over.

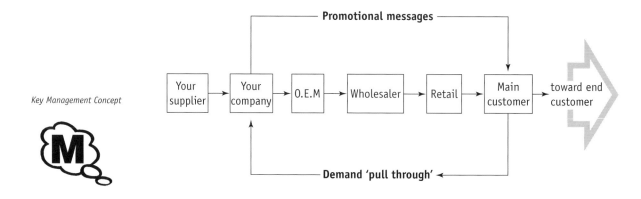

Key Management Concept

Figure 4.17: A channel 'pull' strategy

Figure 4.17 above sets out a simplified 'pull' strategy. In principle the marketing producer company communicates downstream direct to the ultimate or the most important customer in their chain so as to raise awareness, desire and demand for his/her product. In consumer markets, mass media advertising is used, e.g. Heinz, Coca Cola, Thompsons Travel etc. In business to business markets this and/or direct mail is used (so as to be more target group specific and focused) e.g. Microsoft, Intel, Nokia, Sage Accounting.

The demand engendered by this promotion causes the important customers to 'demand' the producer's products from their suppliers and accept no substitutes. Thus the supplier, hopefully, has no choice but to supply the product demanded and demand the same from their suppliers in their turn, and so on up the chain.

One of the key behavioural dimensions of distribution channel management is *leadership*, because in inter-organisational relationships a producer does not enjoy *control* via ownership. However, the company will still desire to be involved with and, in many cases, give direction to, channel members.

The key characteristic of inter-organisational relationships such as those between a manufacturer and an intermediary is *mutual dependence*. Fundamentally, the dealer depends upon the manufacturer for good products, the manufacturer depends upon the dealer for value-added services.

Most companies assume that it is the manufacturer/producer who has the initiative and can invent and take control of their route to market. However, with the possible exception of (so called) direct marketing, (*aka database marketing*) and the increasing use of the Internet in business to business markets, companies requiring a 'route to market' often find the decision taken for them. Channels are often already in place and are confirmed by the buying behaviours of the various customer sets along the way.

Key Learning Point

It is only in the early days of a market that the infrastructure is immature and fragmented enough to allow all and sundry to try their own thing. Michael Dell and PC World could not be established from scratch today. The more mature a market is, the more entrenched are its channels and their infrastructure.

Firms in mature markets either 'go with the flow', or (only if they are rich enough) pioneer entirely novel channels such as did many of the Financial Services companies (Virgin, First Direct, Direct Line) or software houses (Lotus [IBM], S.A.P., Sun Microsystems, et al), even cosmetics (Avon).

Indeed, so powerful are 'channels' in mature markets that they can often select those offerings they wish to 'carry' and refuse all others – (*those so refused will often fail*). It is not unknown in some markets for the more powerful channel members to drive the product development and R&D of their suppliers in order to give themselves a competitive advantage (*this is a trend most prevalent in consumer markets, though not unknown in those dealing in business to business*).

Who controls the channel is a function of who has the power and the initiative. Real power in markets comes via the size of the volume, value and customer loyalty for the given producer's type of products (i.e. the derived demand within the 'food chain'). The greater the combination (of these factors) the more power (and thus potential control) is in the hands of the producer. If these companies take the initiative they will become the (so-called) 'channel captain' and they will be able, via promotion, to have the end customers '**PULL**' the product through the pipeline.

If the market is fragmented so that the combination (of these factors) does not represent a substantial proportion of the channel's business, the most powerful intermediary (not necessarily the largest) will become the channel's captain. In this case intermediaries will exercise their initiative by playing one supplier off against another, thus driving the supply in the direction they want (often lower prices, faster delivery, less work for them, 'better' specifications – i.e. into commodity markets).

In such circumstances the options open to the supplier are highly constrained, the two most open being either:

- to adopt an active sales '**PUSH**' strategy – hoping to load the intermediary's stockrooms and soak up lots of their cash thus encouraging them to sell on down the chain (but intermediaries will be very wary of this happening)

  OR

Key Management Concept

- to go direct to the 'end' customer. This ploy violates the intermediary's belief that customers downstream belong to them, NOT to the supplier. This will produce a great deal of ill will, friction and conflict in the chain, and may even mean that the chain, often *en masse*, will boycott that supplier, leaving the 'direct route' their **only** route to market.

Power in the chain

Whenever dependence exists in a relationship both parties will typically attempt to exercise *power* over each other. The marketer needs to understand the nature of such power, how it is gained, how and when it is exercised and so on.

Any power will be derived from one or a combination of the following classical sources – they are:

1. Legitimate

2. Expert

3. Referent

4. Reward

5. Coercive

Legitimate power is based in law, typically within a tightly defined contract. In this context the roles of channel members are clearly defined and rules and regulations are written down in detail. Control actions will generally be based on deviations from contractual obligations. This power base is a very common feature of *franchised* distribution channels.

Expert power is based on knowledge, typically related to technology although marketing and financial skills are sometimes also significant. To be effective, this power base must be perceived as being *credible*, the strength of the power base being related to the exclusivity of the knowledge base.

Referent power is amongst the strongest of the power bases, yet it is also the least tangible. Fundamentally, it is based on trust and respect, both of which can only be built up over time, i.e. when one party works in the joint best interest of all others.

Reward power is principally based on performance-related inducements, for example, bonuses for achieving specific targets. This power base also embraces non-financial rewards such as training, marketing supports, business advice, goodwill and so on. Reward power is closely related to referent power and often uses expert power (in the form of training etc.) as part of the overall reward package.

Coercive power is founded on the threat that if something is not done then a punishment of some form will be exercised. The premises of this is 'do this or else…' Coercive power is often closely related to legitimate power in the sense that it is typically enforceable with reference to a contract.

An important aspect of dependency relationships is the principle of *countervailing power*. People in organisations react to power by building a defence against it, particularly if the *exercised power* is perceived to be unfair or oppressive. All five bases of power will elicit some form of countervailing power. The strongest resistance is typically against coercive power, particularly where its use is seen as oppressive or its *legitimacy* is not accepted. A typical reaction to unacceptable power exercised by one member of the chain, will be for the others to 'cheat', and this adds inefficiencies to the 'route' and raises its costs. Absence of cheating in a Japanese Kiretzue ensures that their supply chains are a powerful source of competitive advantage.

Channel atmosphere

This is a concept which links levels of *satisfaction* to the degree of *consensus* which exists within the channel relationship. The predominant use of reward power creates an atmosphere of satisfaction and consensus which, in turn, leads to high levels of *co-operation* within channel relationships.

Conversely, the predominant use of coercive power typically generates an atmosphere of dissatisfaction and dissent which, in turn, leads to high levels of *conflict* within channel relationships.

High performance supply chains exist where a *positive* atmosphere and *co-operation* between channel members underpins the relationship. *Low performance* supply chains exist where a *negative* atmosphere and *conflict* between channel members is the norm.

Exercise

Activity

1. Say how you are reaching the 'end customer' that you had in mind in Chapter 2.

2. What are the alternative routes to market?

3. What are the 'pros' – i.e. what value do/would your middlemen add to the equation?

4. What are the 'cons' – i.e. what costs and inconveniences do these intermediaries cause?

5. Evaluate three and four – and if it indicates a change then postulate how you could change channels – and before you act – ask yourself how much the change could cost both directly and in terms of lost, bewildered or dissatisfied customers – (both end customers and middlemen along the way).

The marketing mix

Marketing promotion and communications

Introduction

Effective marketing communications with your customers are essential for business success. The most customer-oriented products in the world will fail if the benefits they deliver are not drawn to the attention of potential buyers, decision makers, specifiers et al.

Equally important is the role of communications *post*-purchase. Everyone is likely to have experienced the situation whereby they look to advertisements to *reinforce* the purchase decision which they have already taken. Communications are central to the marketing process. Established marketing practice proposes the notion of a *communications mix* (see Figure 4.18 on page 182). The customer provides the focus of this mix. It is absolutely essential that communications are closely tailored towards clearly defined target markets and members of the decision making unit (DMU).

Understanding marketing communications

A definition of the communications mix is:

Key Learning Point

> 'A number of *promotional methods* used in *combination* to promote a particular product through *communicating* with individuals, groups and organisations in the 'target group'.

The first point to note is the emphasis on *promotional methods*. There are many ways to get across a range of messages about a product or a company. Successful communications programmes are based on sound judgements as to which techniques should be employed.

The way in which different communications tools are *combined* is also very important. At a product launch, for example, companies will strive to obtain publicity and they will undertake heavy advertising. They may also run sales promotions to encourage trial and the sales force will be deployed to demonstrate and explain the product's benefits. If timing allows, the new product may feature heavily at major exhibitions.

The emphasis on communications draws attention to one of the key problems when developing promotional campaigns. A company must convey a particular message. The customer meanwhile receives the message. The challenge is to ensure that the message sent is interpreted as the sender intended. This simple statement belies the complexity of the task. Communications suggest a two-way exchange of information, this is rarely achieved. Advertising for example, is almost entirely a passive medium. In business markets this problem is being addressed by key account management programmes and a trend towards relationship marketing.

The 'D.A.G.M.A.R' model:

D efine

A dvertising

G oals for

M easured

A dveRtising success.

The horizontal axis within Figure 4.18 provides a model of the communication process we have to take prospects through and constantly reinforce with existing customers. The five stages run from unawareness through to favourable action (*which initially may be a specific sale or contract, then moves on to continuing goodwill and business retention*).

Key Learning Point

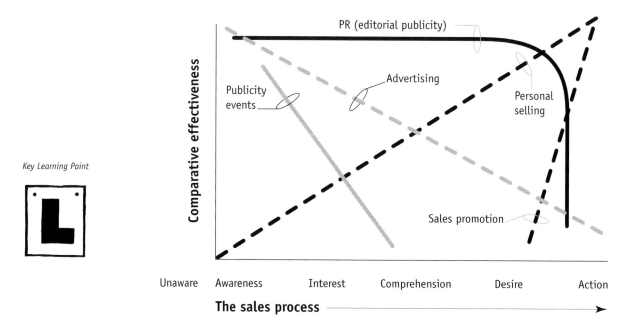

Figure 4.18: The 'D.A.G.M.A.R' model

The key tasks that promotional activities must achieve are:

- Generating sufficient impact to create high levels of awareness and interest within the target group.

- Communicating more tailored messages, which meet specific information requirements, and allow a full understanding of the offering.

- Providing appropriate mechanisms (*such as references, visits to other customer sites, trials or demonstrations*), which strengthen belief and credibility.

- Final convincing processes, normally via sales contact, to secure a favourable decision and to keep a 'happy customer'.

A number of promotional tools and approaches can be useful at each of these stages.

Public relations and editorial publicity (PR & EP)

One of the least well exploited tools or approaches is public relations and a subset of this known as editorial publicity (*i.e. where a 'story' appears about your company within the editorial text of the publication*).

Key Management Concept

Firstly, we need to challenge two publicity myths:

i)   that publicity is free

ii) that all publicity is good publicity.

A write-up on a new product in a prestigious trade magazine is, on the surface, free of charge to the company undertaking the launch. Successful companies, however, put extensive resources into ensuring that the right magazines publish the right stories at the right time. In other words, publicity should be managed and appropriate resources should be allocated to the process.

There are really two strands to PR and EP:

•   one is the promotional, where PR and EP is part of the positive-proactive marketing strategy of the company, and

•   the other where PR and EP is used to lessen the (potentially) damaging effect on the company's image. This is often known as 'crisis PR'.

When the Exxon Valdez crashed into the Alaskan coastline the ensuing outrage badly damaged the company's reputation and sales levels. When a consumer terrorist 'spiked' Heinz baby foods with broken glass, sales of the company's remaining 'varieties' were badly hit. In the first example the company was found to be at fault; in the second, the company was found blameless. In both cases the blaze of negative publicity had a severe impact on the companys' financial performance and brand reputation.

Contrast both of these with the prompt action that Tylenol took when a maniac tampered with packs inserting cyanide capsules

OR

when British Midland showed particular care and attention when one of its planes crash landed on the M1.

As a result of the professional PR in response to these incidents both companies quickly bounced back into favour with their customers.

With the media constantly seeking negative information, companies should endeavour to manage the publicity function professionally, ensuring that it is fully resourced and geared towards achieving consistency with other communications mix components.

On a more positive note, publicity can be extraordinarily powerful, especially when customers perceive it to be an *independent* source of information with respect to products or companies.

The role of advertising and promotion

Key Management Concept

Advertising forms the central plan of most communications programmes. A principal promotional objective is to *convey information* – as the American Advertising Association once remarked, 'Nobody likes advertisements until they require information'.

The information conveyed in advertisements may be in the form of words or symbols. It can work to educate, persuade or simply to inform. An image can be supported or created, enquiries can be elicited and the functions of a product can be demonstrated.

A key role of all promotion, especially advertising, is to *reinforce* a purchase decision i.e. to provide post-purchase reassurance. We see this behind the large majority of trade press business to business marketing communications.

Traditionally, international business has tended to be operated on a *multi-domestic* basis. Nowadays, however, the trend is towards *global* marketing, a factor being recognised by support service organisations such as advertising agencies. Companies at the forefront of globalisation can exploit this fact to create more efficient and effective communications campaigns.

What advertising and promotion cannot do

Many 'lay people' confuse advertising with marketing, the majority seeing the two words as interchangeable. More generally, the perception of many people is that marketing equates to *image creation*.

Advertising is far more likely to *reinforce* rather than *create* a good image. A strong image, meanwhile, is a function of the positive experiences which people have with a product or company. Attempts to create a positive image, while providing poor products or services, are likely to make customers cynical, a problem made worse by negative word-of-mouth.

A common mistake made in advertising is the tendency to *over promise*. While a creative advertisement may make a consumer buy a product once to try it, it cannot force them to repurchase. Thus, if a product does not deliver on the promise made in the advertisement this too will create resentment and negative feelings.

Advertising cannot *reverse long-term decline* nor *change basic product dislike*. It can reinforce loyalty, but not *build* it. To be effective, each element of the promotion mix must form part of a clear strategy and in turn be a constituent part of a coherent marketing mix.

Although it is important to explore the limitations of advertising, the power of this communications element should not be underestimated. Far too often advertising is considered as a cost, not an investment. Worse still, it tends to be treated as a *discretionary* cost.

'I know that half the money I spend on advertising works. Unfortunately I don't know which half'. This famous quote draws attention to a key problem when allocating resources for promotion expenditure, especially advertising. In investment terms, a market cannot forecast a 'hard' return on advertising expenditure in the same way as, for example, one can for a machine for production.

However, all marketing communications should always be considered in a strategic context. The company should explicitly recognise the role of marketing communications in creating and sustaining a key *barrier* to competitors entering the company's market.

Comparing advertising with personal selling

Key Management Concept

The contrast given in the 'D.A.G.M.A.R' model (on page 182) summaries the typical situations when either advertising or personal selling tends to dominate the communications mix. The factors given are a combination of *external* (market) forces and *internal* (organisational) constraints.

As a rule personal selling cannot substitute for 'promotion' or visa versa. On the contrary advertising and personal selling can often be mutually supportive. Personal selling commonly predominates in business to business markets with advertising and promotion playing a supportive role. As opposed to a consumer goods market where advertising predominates with personal selling being used to persuade retailers to provide the company's products with high quality shelf space.

Generally, advertising predominates where a message is relatively simple and/or is intended to reinforce a purchase decision. Advertising is a comparatively *passive* medium which lends itself to these tasks.

However, personal selling predominates where the message is complex, the product/technology has to be demonstrated or when customers have to be informed and 'educated'. Personal selling is an *active* and *interactive* medium which is essential when such an *exchange* of information is required.

There are a number of trends which affect the personal selling role in business to business markets – in particular the emphasis on the growing complexity and sophistication of the purchasing process. In an environment where companies are dramatically reducing their supply base the sales emphasis is increasingly moving towards *relationships* and away from *transactions*.

The communications challenge

It is clear that communications play a fundamental role in the marketing process. Customers are *attracted* to the products of a supplier by their perceptions of the value they will derive from them. They are *retained* by the ongoing satisfactions which they receive from their relationship with that supplier and its products. Communications have a key role in *representing* value and *reinforcing* purchase decisions. The critical problem is that buyers have incomplete knowledge. As a consequence, they are forced into making *judgements* about products and companies. The *communications challenge* is to foster favourable perceptions and reinforce these over time.

Key Learning Point

Once customers are *aware* of a given product (or brand), they can be persuaded to understand its appropriateness in meeting their needs, after which they can be *convinced* of this superiority. The communications challenge is to establish *credibility* in the face of natural customer reticence.

Once the purchase is made, the principal focus of promotion must be on maintaining loyalty. Sales promotions should be focused on loyalty bonuses, e.g. frequent flyer schemes. Advertising will be focused on positive reinforcement of purchase decisions. Personal selling will focus on relationships in general and key account management in particular.

Activity No. 7

Closing the communication gap

Briefing

As per Figure 4.19 on page 190, this exercise identifies 'communication gaps' in a business unit's marketing programme. The starting point is to identify a target market segment and to evaluate its needs in terms of a ranked list of benefits. An objective evaluation of how the company thinks it performs in meeting these benefits is then undertaken, the aim being to benchmark against a 'best-in-class' rival. The exercise has six stages:

1. Name a clearly defined target market segment.

2. Name a 'best-in-class' rival who competes in this segment.

3. Identify the top four key benefits which are sought by customers in your most important target market segment. Rank them in order of priority.

4. Rate how well **you think your company performs** in meeting these benefits. As a benchmark, use the identified 'best-in-class' rival (as per Chapter 2). For measurement purposes use a seven point scale, ranging from -3 to +3. A score of zero states that you are no better or no worse than other companies in meeting the identified benefits. A negative score suggests that you are worse, while a positive score indicates superior performance.

Use the full seven point scale and make the measurement for each customer benefit listed in Stage 3.

Now:

5. Rate how well you think that ***customers* feel that your company performs** in meeting the benefits they seek. Use the same seven point scale and benchmark against the same rival. Once again, a score of zero states that you are no better or no worse than other companies in meeting the identified benefits. A negative score suggests that you are worse, a positive score indicates superior performance.

6. Make the measurement for each customer benefit listed in Stage 3.

7. Evaluate the 'gaps' between the company's perception of its own performance and the perception of its customers.

The output of the exercise can best be expressed in the form of a matrix as shown on the following page.

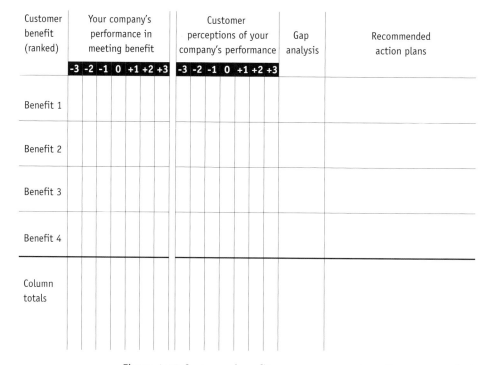

Customer benefit (ranked)	Your company's performance in meeting benefit							Customer perceptions of your company's performance							Gap analysis	Recommended action plans
	-3	-2	-1	0	+1	+2	+3	-3	-2	-1	0	+1	+2	+3		
Benefit 1																
Benefit 2																
Benefit 3																
Benefit 4																
Column totals																

Figure 4.19 Customer benefits – your company's performance analysis

Action Checklist

The final stage is to generate a detailed list of action plans which address the issues raised in the gap analysis. There will be three broad categories of task to be undertaken:

1. Actions relating to the technical and augmented product dimensions of your company's market offering. These will be required when scores in column two are negative or zero.

2. Actions relating to 'communications' dimensions of marketing. These tasks are essential in situations where the company performs well in meeting customer benefits but where it is felt that customers do not perceive this to be the case, i.e. where scores in column three are negative or zero.

3. Priority actions where the company significantly under-performs on the product concept dimensions **and** customers' perceptions are strongly negative.

In this scenario scores in both columns will be negative or zero, indicating that radical solutions regarding the product concept and extensive communications programmes are essential.

The campaign design process

The following text and accompanying mind map being built, set out step-by-step the process of designing a promotions campaign.

A workbook is included in the appendix to act as a guide when the reader first sets out to put this next section into practice.

Key Management Concept

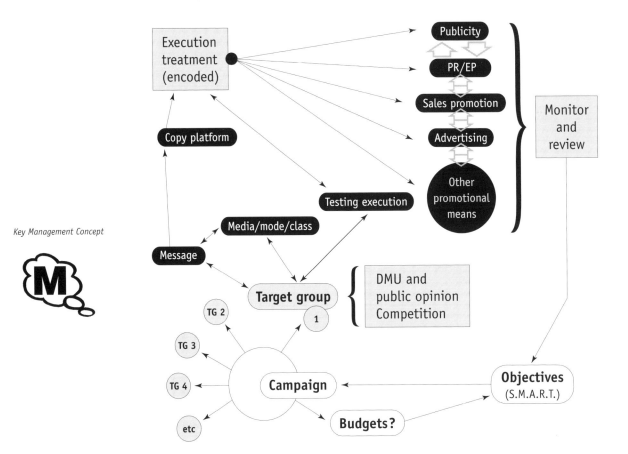

Figure 4.20: Building a campaign

Figure 4.20 (*opposite*) is a mind map of the basic campaign design process. It is a cycle of events starting with the dialogue, that is the budget and objective setting process, then proceeding clockwise via the selection of the target group, choosing the class of promotion, the messages that will need to be transmitted, how these messages will be treated creatively to improve impact and retention by the target audience, deciding the best promotional mix, to the essential step of monitoring the promotion's progress, and measuring its success at the end. We will build this mind map step-by-step in the final parts of this chapter.

The 'foundation stones'

When the marketer first starts to design a promotional campaign there are three 'foundation stones' that must fit together intimately. They are:

- the campaign **objectives**
- the **campaign** design and
- the **budgets** to pay for it.

Action Checklist

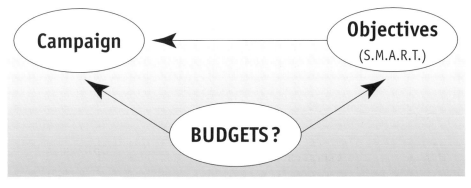

Figure 4.21: The campaign's foundation stones

Like their masonry counterparts, they are married by a process of tailoring each in turn so that they fit together as closely as possible. Ideally the process starts with the objectives, i.e. an idea of what the marketer would like the campaign to achieve. However, often the marketer is presented with the budgets first and has now to see what campaign this will afford and what can be achieved with it.

If we deal with the ideal world first then we will know what to strive toward.

Objectives

Promotional objectives are not the same as the business objectives of the company, but they are derived from them, via the specific marketing objectives that relate to this campaign.

Action Checklist

The relationship is:

    Business objectives

        Marketing objectives

            Role of promotions in the mix

                Promotions objectives

                    Objectives for each part of the promotions mix to be employed.

An example of this cascade relationship would be:

- **Business objective**
  'To improve our return on capital employed by gaining economies of scale'.

- **Marketing objective to serve this:**
  'To increase our market share by two percentage points per year over the next five years'.

The role of promotion will be to generate leads for the sales force to follow up, **and** to improve the target group's awareness of our products' 'differential advantage'.

- **Advertising objective**
  'To generate 200 high quality leads per month over the next year'.

- **PR/EP objective**
  'To raise awareness of our competitive differential advantage (CDA) by six percentage points per year over the next five years'.

These objectives, like any other, are most useful when they are **S.M.A.R.T**:

S pecific

M easurable

A greed

R ealistic

T ime based

Specific

Quite clear and unambiguous, easily identifiable, such as in this case: to raise the level of awareness in the target audience.

Measurable

'What you don't measure you can't manage', in this case, awareness can be measured before, and compared to, the measurement of its level after the campaign.

Agreed

Like all managers, marketers achieve their objectives through other people, some in their teams, some outside. What is not agreed will not be 'bought into' and therefore will not have the team's support.

Realistic

People will only give their support to something on which their performance will be measured, if that something is realistic.

Time based

This sets the deadline by which time the objective should be attained. Lateness equals failure, promptness or being early equals success.

An example of a **S.M.A.R.T** objective is:

> 'To increase the level of awareness for brand 'x' by 3% over the next six months'.

The key issues are that promotional objectives should:

- specify results that can reasonably be expected from promotion

- be based on a reasonable analysis of the best available facts and judgements

- be bench marked for measurement (*i.e. where did you start from, what are promotions of other products doing, what sort of results emanate from others in your field, particularly the competition*), **and**

- noted in written, **S.M.A.R.T** terms.

Budgets

One of the most persistent questions any marketing consultant gets is:

How much should we be spending on our advertising?

Key Question

The assumption always is that there is a magic percentage (of sales, gross or net profit), which may vary from industry to industry, but which, if applied to the questioner's company, will ensure success.

No such 'magic' ratio has ever been shown to exist. However, this is still how many companies set their promotional budgets:

i) as a percentage of last year's sales/profit etc. (at least the company knows it has that money)

ii) as a percentage of anticipated sales/profit for this year, (let's hope the spend is enough, yet not too much).

Both these methods fall into the trap set for them by either the business cycle and/or the product life cycle (PLC).

Consider the following curve:

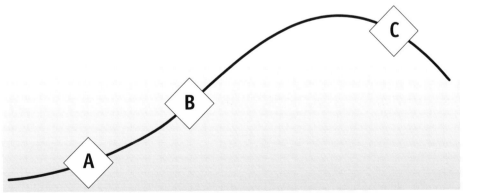

Key Management Concept

Figure 4.22: Part of any business cycle or product life cycle

If the curve is a PLC, at point 'A' any percentage of sales, particularly last years, will not be enough. At this stage of a product's life it needs all the support it can get, particularly if it has as yet to 'cross the chasm' (see Chapter 3). Points 'B' and 'C' apply whatever the cycle. At point 'B' the amount as a percentage of business, thus set aside for promotion will clearly not be enough to support the rising market. At point 'C' the amount will obviously be too much and much of it will be wasted. Indeed, if this is a PLC, perhaps any spend will be wasted. It's like Canute trying to turn back the tide. Many successful product managers would cut all expenditure, not just promotion, and 'put the product into the dairy to milk it too death' as a means of raising the necessary investment for those products that are before the curve.

Another favourite way to set a promotions budget is:

iii) 'Share of voice'

In this approach the amount spent by the competition is used as a sort of yard stick. This amount can be arrived at via the services of several agencies, the most well-known being MEAL (*Media Expenditure Analysis Ltd*). They derive a ballpark figure by tracking what each of the major companies in an industry commission in terms of media time (if broadcast) or space (if printed) and extrapolating via the rate cards for the media used.

This method is beloved of advertising agencies – they will advocate 'share of voice' strategies, such that if you want to gain market share, surely you must spend more than the main competitors; if you just want to hold your own, you can't afford to spend less, etc.

Finally, there is the so-called:

iv) 'Objective and task' method

This gets as close to the ideal as one can. The principle is that the budget setting process starts by costing the campaign which needs to be employed to achieve the original objectives. This is then compared with the reality of what the company can afford. A dialogue now takes place in which the objectives are 'shaved down' in some places and these shavings traded for budget increases in other areas of promotion, so as to arrive at the best compromise.

The campaign

The main issues to be addressed in any promotional campaign and in the following order are:

- Objectives (as examined above)
- Target groups
- Mode (or 'class') strategy
- Media strategy
- Message (*i.e. the 'copy platform'*)
- Creative execution
- Testing methods
- Monitoring and measurement.

We will now examine these in order (this is the order employed by the workbook appended). As we proceed we will build the mind map which started this section Figure 4.20, and the triumvirate of objectives, budgets and campaign, Figure 4.21 being the starting block.

The target group

The quintessential issue is a clear definition of the target group.

Key Management Concept

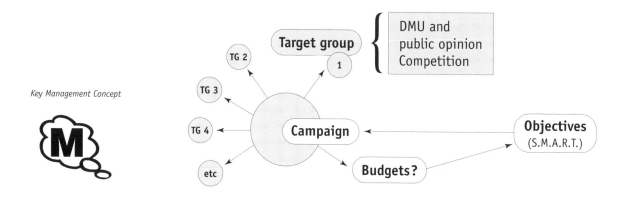

Figure 4.23: The target group

Which group of people does the marketer wish to address? These are defined in consumer markets by their demography (i.e. age, gender, race, lifestyle, location, 'socio-economic group', as per Chapter 3 etc.). In business to business markets, they will additionally be defined by their position in the DMU, (*e.g. specifier, decider, user, etc.*). In any communication, in addition to the target audience, there is the matter of the wider public, which will often be a party to the communication (anything more person specific is more sales, than promotion). It is well to remember that the competition will also be listening-in to the campaign.

A campaign may have several target groups, sometimes these can be so dissimilar that they cannot be adequately reached, and the desired message clearly communicated, without treating them as a discrete audience. If this is the case, as can be seen in Figure 4.23 above, they should be the basis of a sub-campaign of their own. For example, in the case of a major company promoting welding rods, the mode, media and the message will be different for the engineering or production directors of shipyards (budget holders), compared to that designed to reach the welders themselves (users).

A definition of the target group or audience, is essential to being able to specify mode/class, and media.

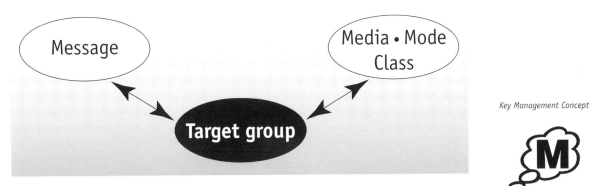

Key Management Concept

Figure 4.24 : Defining the target group

Mode/class

What mode, or class of promotion is the company going to use? By this we mean, is it going to be advertising, PR/EP, exhibitions, seminars, Internet, direct mail hospitality, visits to reference sites etc.

Media

This defines whether the channel of communication will be via:

Key Management Concept

- printed media such as the press, or posters, or
- broadcast media such as radio, television, or commercials breaking into mobile phone conversations as in Sweden etc.

By getting close to the intended audience the marketer will be able to divine the modes and classes of promotion to which the audience is open, and which media they 'consume' (i.e. not just reception via circulation, but they read, digest and internalise the content e.g. lots of people in the higher socio-economic groups buy both *The Sun* and *The Financial Times*, but when it comes to financial and business editorial they will give more credit to the latter and less to the former. When it comes to sport it may be the other way around). This 'closeness' derives either from the use of market research or longer-term customer information systems (see Chapter 7).

Media choices

There are two distinct decisions to be made about the choice of media:

- the *inter* media choice and

- the *intra* media choice.

Action Checklist

First – 'inter media', this is the decision whether to use, and in what combination, **the media of**:

- Radio

- Television

- National press

- Local press

- Direct mail

- Posters

- Sponsorship, etc...

Comparing each for their factors in choice:

Action Checklist

- Reach
- Creative scope
- Sales history
- Cost re the budget
- Reaction of the 'trade'
- Flexibility of booking
- Competitor's use
- Security/confidentiality, etc.

Second the 'intra media' choice, i.e. how do different vehicles within a class of media compare in terms of:

Action Checklist

- Cost
- Coverage
- Atmosphere
- Credibility
- Context
- Frequency
- Reproductive quality etc.

Message

As can also be seen from Figure 4.23, (page 200) familiarity with the target group is also necessary for the marketer to be able to define the message. A different message will be sent to the production director (decider/ budget holder) than that sent to the welder (user) e.g. to the director/decider = 'High production rates with less wastage' – whereas to the welder/user = 'Less fumes, less chance you will suffer from 'welder's' lung'.

Key Management Concept

The message exists in two distinct forms:

- **First** – the creative strategy, sometimes referred to as the 'copy platform', which is a succinct plain English term of what needs to be communicated.

- **Then** – the creative execution or treatment, which is how the copy platform will be translated so as better to be absorbed, understood and effect the behaviour of the target group (i.e. it is in their language and their emotional 'set').

Key Learning Point

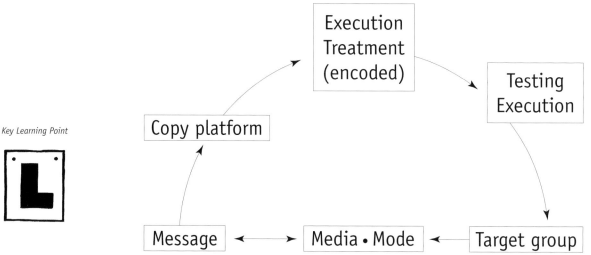

Figure 4.25: The sequence

The sequence is portrayed in Figure 4.25. To illustrate this take the consumer example of the classic promotion of Heinz baked beans back in the late 1970s. Research showed that mums in middle socio-economic groups were feeling that baked beans were a food associated with hard times, and that now their families were a little more affluent, should they not give their children something better?

So the copy platform designed by the marketer/product manager, was based on the need for these mums to obtain peer group reassurance that baked beans were a fine food for growing children, irrespective of the lower costs.

Across the several campaigns the associated copy platform read, something along the lines of:

- 'Don't feel you are serving lower quality food to your growing family, a lot of other mums also buy Heinz baked beans'.

The various treatments/executions (*not in order*) featured 'hook-lines' such as:

- 'Beanz builds a body' (yes, with a 'z', see later).
- 'A million housewives every day, pick up a tin of beanz and say, Beanz means Heinz' (this sung to a catchy tune).

Later abbreviated to just:

- 'Beanz meanz Heinz'.
- 'You know what beanz meanz'

The campaign went out using press posters and television. The ads always featured aspirational mums and bouncy healthy pre-teen children. The campaign was such a success, that even today, some twenty or more years later, one only has to hum the tune or quote the start of the 'hook-line' and many people can complete it for you.

Creative strategy

The copy platform: i.e. what the marketer wants the promotion to say, there are a great deal of propositions that can be put to a market. Some of the classic types are listed below:

Where the propositions lie:

Product – service characteristics

- Constituents
- Performance in use
- Presentation
- Availability (or parity)
- Versatility
- Country of origin

User characteristics

- Celebrities or known experts
- Most sports competitors use it
- Only 'the best' use it

Price characteristics

- Lasts longer
- Reassuringly more expensive
- Payment more convenient

Image characteristics

- Quality
- Good value
- Friendly to you
  - To community
  - To environment
  - To country's economy, etc.
- Contemporary

Disadvantages of non-use

- Resultant suffering e.g. loss of status
  - Client
  - Profit
  - Job
- Missed opportunity

Direct comparisons with competitors

- Product comparison
- 'Knocking copy'
- Parody competitor's advertising, slogans, origins etc.

Ways of using the product/ service

- Philanthropic
- Caring for the community/ environment
- Responsible citizen

How the service is/ was developed

Surprising facts about the product

- Technology
- Responsibility
- Mind boggling numbers

Satisfies psychological/ physiological needs

- Thirst
- Hunger
- Loneliness

- Sex
- Social confidence
- Being a good: mum, dad, citizen etc.

Product heritage

- Comes from Finland (etc.)
- Established 1865
- Founders of the company

Newsworthiness

- New, improved
- Anniversaries
- Topical events

Generic benefits

- Appropriate a characteristic of all the market to yourself e.g. for Nokia *'Connecting people'*

Boost sales force morale

- Is there a better way to do it?

Increase traffic

Increase trade activity

Creative execution/treatment

There are some important principles which should be borne in mind when either designing the treatment, briefing an agency to design one for the company, or evaluating one that has been offered to the company. These are:

Is the campaign to be 'burst' or 'drip'?

Usually, a combination of the two. A 'burst' campaign is one where an intense amount of promotional activity takes place over a very short period of time. Often the campaign will involve coordinated combinations of classes and types of media. For example, television ads with posters, articles in the press and on the broadcast news, sampling opportunities and perhaps even direct mail; nowadays it often involves the launch of a web site or web page.

The aim of a 'burst' campaign is, via a higher than normal share of voice, to raise awareness and understanding within the target group. Once a 'burst' has raised awareness, if this is not supported, it is soon forgotten as it is drowned out by the noise of competitive activity (it is said that in the UK the average person is subjected to some 1,200+ different promotional messages every week).

A 'drip' campaign is designed to ensure that the company's name or proposition is not forgotten. It will normally focus on name awareness, and evocation of the original 'burst'. It can feature such ploys as the use of name boards facing the television cameras at a football or rugby match, or the use of a catch phrase (*Beanz Meanz Heinz*), or a tune such as 'Jesu joy of man's desiring' which is used to advertise a major brand of cigars.

Design the whole campaign to achieve 'V.I.P.S'.

This stands for:

V isibility

I dentity

P romise

S implicity

Visibility

There is no point in spending a great deal of money on promotion if it is invisible to the intended audience.

Identity

This means that there should always be a consistent style about the promotion, whatever the mode, class or medium, by which, without the advertiser explicitly saying so, the audience can tell who it's from.

Promise

What is the proposition to the customer? What is the promise that will be delivered if only they would buy, use, or otherwise get others to do so?

Simplicity

The principle here is that each episode, advertisement, aspect of the promotion will be at its most effective when the message is simple, direct and to the point. One message at a time should be the aim, remember **K.I.S.S**: 'Keep It Simple Stupid'.

Testing the execution

Referring again to Figure 4.25 (page 204), it can be seen that the final stage before going live with the campaign is to test the execution to ensure that it does communicate what is intended.

It is normally impossible to pre-test promotion in such a way that the propensity to buy (etc.) can be measured. Even if the testing involves focus group discussions, answers to the question, 'Would you buy this?' are very unreliable. Issues such as wishing to please the host, or wishing to go along with the others in the group, are a phenomenon that is known as 'risky shift'* gets in the way. So the canny marketer will use other tools to measure interest without it becoming apparent that this is what is happening. Such tools are employed in a 'laboratory' context although sometimes the laboratory is no more grand than a 'hall test'.

Testing tools fall under the three headings of:

Physiological

- Pupil dilation
- Eye movement
- Heart beat
- Pulse rate

Oral/written responses

- Attention, noting
- Awareness
- Recall, comprehension
- Interest
- Liking
- Attitude expressed involvement (e.g. handling)

Behavioural

- Coupon response
- Token money in 'shop'
- Gift choice

> *   'Risky shift' is where people in a group are more likely to accept risk than they would be if on their own, so in this context it is manifest by people saying they liked something, or would buy it, when they are with the group, but when they are on their own this would be the last thing they would do.

This stage is normally difficult, but is particularly hard when testing completely new concepts and messages. Both the Benson & Hedges and the Heineken campaigns scored zero in the initial market research because those tested said that it was not real advertising. However, both became loved by their respective audiences eventually, when they had 'caught-on'.

So, when the testing results look encouraging enough, the campaign goes into the field.

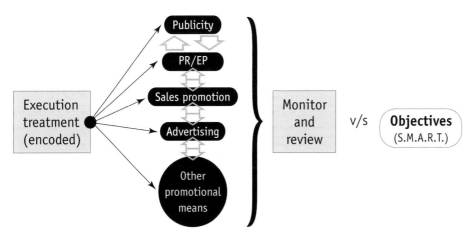

Figure 4.26: The campaign

The main issue in Figure 4.26 is that the marketer must monitor the performance of the campaign in real time. There are two reasons for this:

- Most importantly, promotion is a black hole into which a great deal of money can be lost. It is too late at the end of the campaign to discover that it did not work. The canny marketer, whilst having confidence in his/her own judgment, and allowing time for the campaign to develop and to work, will also be looking to spot signs of danger so that the campaign can be corrected early on, or pulled if it is beyond repair, before too much money has gone down the drain.

   The second reason is that the campaign should always be treated as a learning opportunity, and thus if the campaign is monitored during, and its results are studied in detail afterwards, valuable lessons will be learned for next time.

The tools to be used to monitor the campaign during its progress and afterwards will depend on what the original S.M.A.R.T objectives were.

They can range from:

- before and after studies of customer/user 'uses and attitudes' toward the product
- sales figures, to
- the propensity for competitor's customers to switch etc.

Thus the campaign has come full circle.

The marketing plan

Chapter 5

Introduction

It is said that: 'Those who fail to plan, are effectively planning to fail', and so it is with marketing. The whole point of marketing planning is to coordinate the efforts of the team, together with the necessary resources, including finance, so it all comes together when and where it is wanted, so as to achieve the desired outcomes for the company.

Key Management Concept

The plan as a working document

The plan must state the performance standards required and agreed (*remember the 'S.M.A.R.T.' acronym for planning the promotional campaign, Chapter 4*), these are expressed as targets for critical success factors, including timings and coordination, and the budgets to achieve them. It must also allocate responsibility to those who must drive its progress. It is usually not the remit of the plan to allocate authority, but the planner must bear in mind that few can discharge a responsibility without the necessary authority, for example to sign off sums of money, to censure those who are expected to act if they fail to do so etc.

The 'fruit' of a plan is its programme (or '*action plan*', but that is confusing, so we will use the word '*programme*' to indicate the document which sets out the actions to be taken, by when and by whom) and this must be drawn with sufficient detail and clarity to enable the marketer, during the period when the plan is current, to monitor where they are, compared to where they want to be. The key elements to check should be available for all to see (*within the bounds of necessary confidentiality*) say up on a wall chart, in diaries and on organisers. It is a total waste of time, effort and money to prepare plans which are then locked away, as so often happens, and which is one of the main reasons why many people don't think planning works. Often such plans have never been implemented because those preparing the plan had neither the remit, skills or authority to delegate the actions the plan required to happen.

The plan as a learning process

Additionally, good planning is a learning process. Planning is not an exact science, especially when dealing with marketplaces which are notoriously dynamic and open systems. Marketers do make mistakes, and like anyone, they need to learn from them. For example: customers and/or competitors don't always oblige by being predictable. To paraphrase an old military axiom: 'No plan survives intact its first contact with reality', the unexpected will always happen.

In these situations it is the existence of a plan that enables the marketer to define where the company should have been, and compare this with where they actually ended up, and learn from the discrepancy. Every time a marketer goes around the planning cycle, from analysis, through synthesis, to implementation and operations, they should get better at the art of planning.

Without a good marketing plan the company is 'rudderless' and instead of seizing and maintaining the initiative by being proactive, it is reactive, and thus allows the competition, customers and suppliers to set the agenda because they will have the initiative instead.

The plan in context

Any plan, particularly one for business, is part of other plans and is also set in the context of the organisation's policies, operational procedures, strategies, mission statements, business and marketing strategies and its strategic vision (be they explicit or implicit, as is so often the case nowadays).

First of all, it is important to understand the relationship between the company's various plans: corporate, business and marketing. Consider Figure 5.1 below:

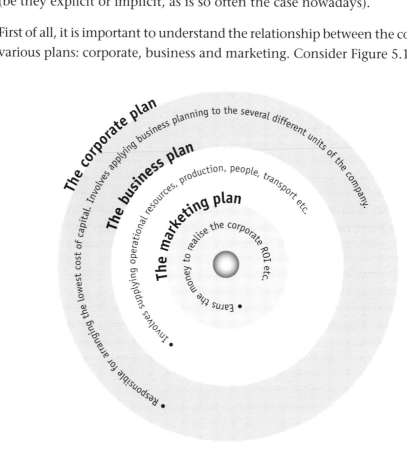

Figure 5.1: The hierarchy of planning

In Figure 5.1 opposite we show the marketing plan nested within the accompanying corporate and business plans. The marketing plan is part of the business plan of the organisation which in turn is part of the overall corporate plan. The Figure shows the focus of each layer.

- **The corporate plan** is looking toward satisfying the needs of those supplying finance to the company, be they shareholders, banks etc. Its main job is to ensure the lowest possible cost of capital available for its use, by maintaining a high rate of return on investments with as low a level of risk as possible.

(*Corporate concerns also involve the nature of the company's image, to all stakeholders not just the financial people – companies are increasingly concerned with being good corporate citizens – and in this pursuit marketing can also make a valuable contribution.*)

- **The marketing plan** is the vehicle via which the cash is earned to make that return on capital. The business plan, of which the marketing plan is part, provides the resource and necessary support, such as production, servicing, transport, people etc. to the cash generation process.

Ideally, the total planning process involves the proposed corporate plan initially setting outline financial goals and budgets directly for the marketing plan to achieve as in Figure 5.2 over.

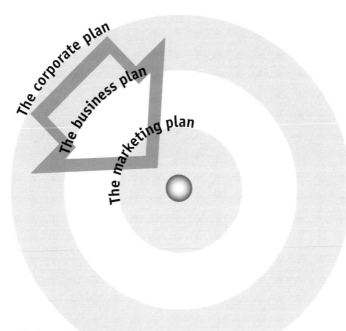

Corporate stipulates the financial
goals of the company and the resource available

Figure 5.2: The hierarchy of planning

Some dialogue may well take place at this juncture, as we will see later it may well be that the revenue required is unrealistic given the state of the business, product range and/or its market. Some strategy may be required to fill the 'gap' that lies between what is required to happen, and what will happen if nothing new is done.

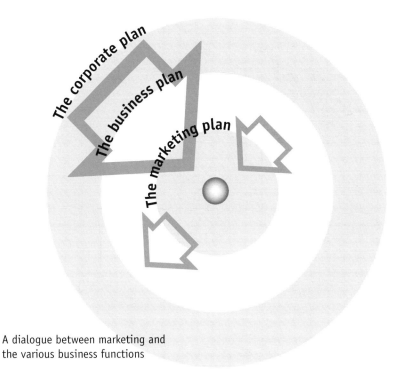

A dialogue between marketing and
the various business functions

Figure 5.3: The hierarchy of planning

At some stage, business planning is involved to ensure that there is a match
between the support required by the revenue earning process and the support
that the business functions can provide. This itself may require further dialogue
with corporate, to either supply more finance or reduce their expectations.

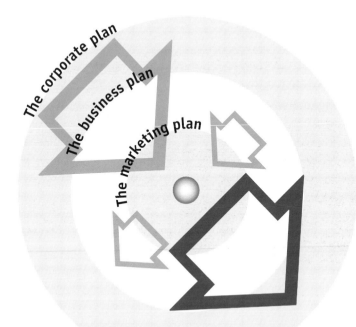

The final dialogue with corporate planning,
re. what is obtainable with resources available

Figure 5.4: The programme formulation stage

Finally as in Figure 5.4 above, the dialogues necessary to arrive at some meetings of minds are concluded and thus the planning process itself can proceed to the programme formulation stage.

The next major context to understand is the way that planning fits into the hierarchy that stretches from 'operations' to 'strategic vision'. We show below the way these elements in the process are nested.

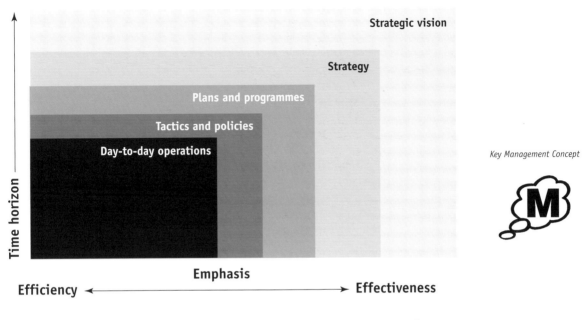

Key Management Concept

Figure 5.5: The context of strategy

The horizontal axis is shown as being a dimension moving from efficiency in the bottom left to, effectiveness at the bottom right. This axis could equally well have shown the increasing seniority of the people involved as the chart moves right. So the junior ranks such as the sales and supervisory people are involved with the discharge of operations and tactics, whilst planning and programmes are the responsibility of middle management and strategy is the concern of senior management and the board of directors.

Moving out from the origin at the bottom left:

When things at the operational 'coal face' are not as expected, and decisions are required, then those involved turn to the operational manuals, which are the repository of tactics and company policy in the sense that these are paradigms for guidance.

(If this happens, then this must be the response, e.g. if a customer asks for a larger discount than they currently enjoy, then up to a certain level, it can only be in return for a stipulated increase in business, faster payment etc. above that level then there must be a special business case put to management who will make the decision.)

When things change to the extent that the operations manual can no longer cope, say a competitor has done something unexpected, then middle management resort to the business or marketing plans and programmes.If this cannot deal with the situation, and the plan needs to be rewritten, then the planners fall back to the strategy for guidance.

The 'strategic vision' is the last resort of a company's decision taking. It should be the bedrock of everything it does. When decisions are taken, a major input is to evaluate which option will serve the vision of the company best, and to favour that course over any other. Some companies, notably Japanese, have strategic visions which look 20 or more years ahead, others are not so far sighted, regrettably too many western companies have no strategic vision at all, even the largest seem often to be driven by quarterly results only.

The marketing programme

When exercising any craft, it is indispensable to have in mind a clear idea of the end product required. So it is with marketing planning. The whole point of the process is to produce a working document that choreographs and co-ordinates the required actions from the marketing and support teams, so as to achieve the plan's intentions. Thus we start our examination in the bottom left of Figure 5.5 above.

Key Management Concept

Mix element	Quarter 1	2	3	4	5	Who takes responsibility?
Budget	£1.8m	£3.15m	£5.3m	£6.2m	£4.8m	
Product						
Market research	New outlet survey	Report and analysis				RC
Modifications			New product modification	Tool-up	Commence production	AJ
New product launch		**Commence planning for launch**			Approve	AJ, RC & MD
Packaging						
New pack development	Concept approval	Finalise test pack		Tool-up	Add to production run	RC & TOM
Research			Test and finalise			TOM
Trials		**Test new pack**				RC
Service support						
Call centre	Customer focus groups	Design	Trials	Approval & set-up		DTH
Training programme		Pilot new customer progs.	Revamp as needed	Run first course	Appraise results	IAC
Price						
Customer finance scheme	Consult with R Branson et al	Consult and design	Delphi test	**Design and launch trials of new scheme**		MD & FAC
New price list	Discussions	Design	Sign-off	Print new lists	In-field	FAC
Repositioning price strategies				**Commission and start market research**		TOM & FAC
Promotion *(excluding media schedules)*						
Main advertising campaign	Outline strategy	Test strategy & approve	Modify as necessary	Start buying media	Main mass media campaign goes live	TC & RC
PR/EP campaign				**Press briefings re. new product**		TC
Sales campaign				Brief sales force	Selling-in	MRB & RC
Distribution						
Market research	Brief and select agency	Focus groups	Main survey			FAC
Existing distributors				**Distributors annual conference**		MRB

Figure 5.6: Outline marketing programme (or action plan)

Sound objectives and an effective strategy are the foundations upon which everything else in the marketing plan is built. To put it into effect requires a detailed plan of implementation, a programme relating events to times, budgets and responsibilities, a fictional illustration of which we show in Figure 5.6.

Action Checklist

Each major action or supporting sub-programme must be organised in terms of:

- detailing the mix of resources to be used
- the timetable of key activities
- setting and agreeing overall targets and budgets for the required results
- identifying, and getting the agreement of the key personnel, to take the responsibility for the requisite actions.

It is good practice to layout the programme visually (*as per Figure 5.6*), to summarise stages and to show the linkages and related deadlines. For simple tasks this can best be done using Gantt charts, but for more complicated programmes especially those requiring a great deal of interdepartmental coordination, network analysis tools such as critical path analysis (CPA) or even PERT may have to be employed.

It is essential that those who are involved in making the plan work are involved as early as practical so that they 'own' the programme, and will thus take responsibility for their part in its implementation. This is of particular relevance to colleagues in the sales force of the company. Their targets, budgets, key deadlines, and business/customer development plans must be fully in line with, and supportive of, the intended marketing programme. The culmination of this stage is the fine tuning and detailed re-negotiation with those concerned to resolve conflicting priorities and finalise budgets.

Developing the marketing plan

Coverage

Companies develop their own formats for what they want to cover in their marketing plans – a comprehensive list is provided on page 234.

Where major brands of the company are concerned, there may be an overall policy document which delineates acceptable marketing activities, so that only fine tuning can take place by the brand manager without approval from the board.

Whatever the situation, there are some general principles of good practice which should be built into any planning process:

All good plans are rooted in reality

As a vital part of the planning process, it is essential to continually conduct a full review of the company's situation in its markets. This is known as the marketing audit and is analogous to a car driver keeping their eyes open at all times whilst on the road. The marketing audit, complete with **SWOT** analysis is so important to the very conduct of marketing that this book devotes the whole of Chapter 6 to this topic.

Firms that start the process with the stipulation of product objectives, fully developed budgets and/or financial targets alone, risk a dislocation from the real world that means it is impossible for the company to be marketing oriented. Consequently there will be very little commitment from the people who have to implement those plans.

Objectives should be unambiguous and clear

Everyone involved should know what is expected of them, and what their contribution to the plan's success must be. S.M.A.R.T-ness in these objectives is to be encouraged (*ref. Chapter 4, Part IV*).

The strategy should be unambiguous and clear

The job of strategy is to state the overall 'game plan' of how the company intends to pursue its goals. This can be expressed as a hierarchy of objectives such as:

- To pursue the long-term vision of the company we will need to dominate our markets.

To do this:

- This year we will need to grow our share by (say) 5%.

To do this:

- We must launch the mark 2 version of the product.

To do this:

- We have to conclude its re-design, get it into production in time to be launched in quarter three.

To launch in quarter three:

- The sales force must be briefed in quarter two, as must our distributors.

To brief the distributors:

- A trade conference should be scheduled for the latter half of quarter two.

However, it is dangerous to confuse the 'what' elements with the 'how' elements. Strategy is the consistent direction of that part of the company's business. Thus, in order not to end up with a series of disjointed and ineffective activities, it is wise, if not essential to pull all the strategic thinking together in one part of the plan (*see Figure 5.9, page 234*).

The strategic section should cover more than just the strategy for the elements of the marketing mix. Although it will be useful to summarise the mix in the strategic section, the main contents must be:

- The overall approach to develop and consolidate the business basis of the product in its market/s.

- The overall customer strategy, what are the sources of revenue, i.e. who are your target group/s, the segments, and how will the total mix offering differ, from one segment to another.

- With what companies will the organisation co-operate, and with whom will it compete, and how.

- The overall product proposition and positioning in its various market places, (*as per Chapter 4, Part I*).

The strategic thinking should be purposeful in the sense that it is designed to be the best overall approach to achieving the goals, after careful consideration of all the options available. Turn the page and consider Figure 5.7.

Key Management Concept

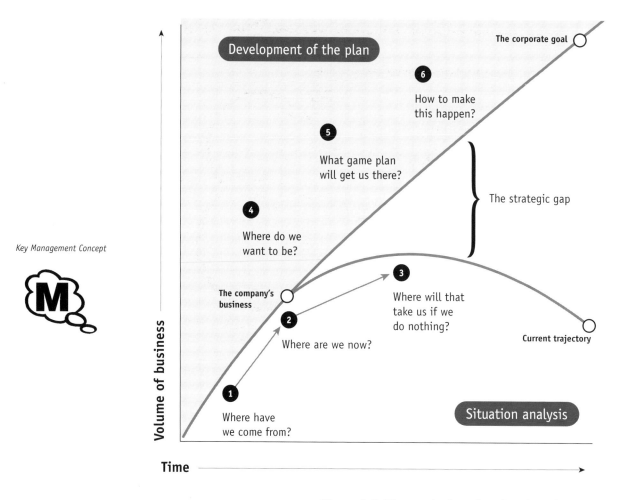

Figure 5.7: The marketing planning thought process

The sorts of marketing strategies that can be adopted are provocatively discussed by the authors Ries and Trout in their book *Marketing Warfare*.

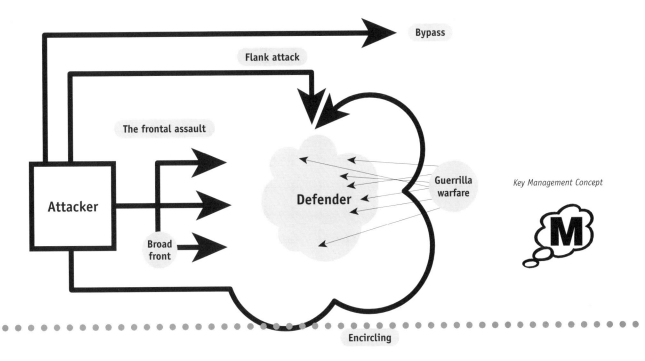

Figure 5.8: The options when taking on the competition

To give an outline of what is involved in these strategies:

The principles of defence

Only the market leader should consider opting for a pure defensive strategy. And even then try to avoid a static/passive defence – it leads to complacency which is a killer.

The best defence is always attack, keep the competitor on the back foot and maintain the initiative at all costs. Forceful competitive moves from the opposition should always be blocked, even if it is believed they have no chance, the fact that they keep trying will gain them a positive reputation, whilst the onlooker companies will seem negative.

Key Management Concept

Key Learning Point

Keep a look-out for potential trouble, if your company is the market leader, it is most likely to come from one of two directions:

- those companies who are close to the size of the leader, and

- those companies that are very small indeed, i.e. those who are cherry picking your market (*see Chapter 3*).

(If it comes from both at the same time this will tempt you to split your forces, always a dangerous thing to do.)

In either case any hostile move must be opposed, particularly the cherry picker, who never seems to be much of a threat until they are well established and thus very difficult to attack. When attacked they are not likely to stand and fight, they know they would lose so there is no point. They are more likely to play the guerrilla, so that whilst the major company is consolidating one cherry, they will be picking another elsewhere whilst the big company is not looking.

Key Learning Point

The principles of defence

If it can be avoided, never attack an opponent on the ground of their own choosing, in the military this is aptly called the 'killing ground'. The artful strategist will always attempt a flanking move, rather than attack head-on. Sometimes, however, a head-on attack cannot be avoided, in that case the strategist must be prepared to take heavy losses, the experts reckon that the attrition rate will be in excess of three to one. i.e. for every pound a company spends defending, the aggressor will have to spend more than three attacking if they are to have any hope of success. The best flanking attack is not to contest an area of the opponent's weakness (never underestimate a competitor, to do so gives them an advantage. They will be quite aware of their weaknesses and will have a contingency prepared – it could even be a trap).

Rather attack a weakness in their strength, where because of their success, their resources are probably already overstretched.

An example of this was the way that Agfa attacked Kodak in the Great Barrier Reef resorts of Queensland, Australia. Photographic film ripens with age, it is too raw to use just after production, and too ripe within a year or so. The hotter the climate, the shorter the period from production to over-ripeness when the film will not take good pictures. The distribution system of Kodak is aimed at getting the film into the customer's hands within a time frame during which its ripeness is acceptable to most photographers.

However, this presupposes proper stock rotation and fairly regular sales at the retail counter which for smaller non photographic outlets cannot be guaranteed.

Kodak is the major photographic brand worldwide, and its success stretches even their professional logistics management. Getting the film in the right place, merchandised on the right stands within the optimum time often happens, but the tropical climate means that the timeframe is smaller than elsewhere. This situation is compounded by the fact that retailers are not that good at the discipline of stock rotation for what they see as a nice, but not critical opportunity purchase, particularly as there is no comeback from the customer if the pictures turn out badly. The 'happy snapper' type of customers are usually not aware that a poor print can be caused by over ripe film not necessarily their poor technique.

There is a class of big spending photographers, however, known to the trade as 'amateur professional'. These people know all about film ripening, and when they can, they prefer to purchase from those retailers who supply professional photographers. In such outlets the film is kept in fridges, and the photographer will do likewise when they are storing their film between purchase and the shoot.

Queensland is a big place, and it is a long way between professional film retailers. So Agfa, even though they are minnows in Australian tourist photography, decided to attack Kodak with a 'professional's film' merchandised in the cool cabinets of grocery outlets throughout the state. The film was more expensive per roll, but totally outsold Kodak to this specific and valuable segment.

Similar strategies could well work when fighting competitors who have totally inadequate call centres, and don't realise the amount of customer frustration this causes. A company that over resourced their call centres and could boast the shortest waiting times, could attract a good many of its competitor's customers.

Such strategies do indeed involve expensive activity, they will not be efficient, but they will be effective, and as we have said, attack is always costly – but never as costly as losing and going bust.

A flank attack

A good flanking attack is made in an area which is so far uncontested. A segment where the customers are discontented, where they can be persuaded that your company could serve them better, in their perception, than they are served currently.

Surprise is always a potent constituent, the less time the competitors have to prepare the better. Once the competitors are on the run, do not let them pause to take breath, keep them off balance, maintain the initiative – the quality and dynamism of the pursuit is as critical as the original attack. Failure to pursue will often mean that the opponent can regroup and re-establish themselves successfully so that in a few short months it is almost like nothing happened and the attacker will have spent a great deal for nothing.

A guerrilla campaign

This is the world of the cherry picker. They attack segments where although there is a gap in the market, to the main player there are no markets in these gaps. These segments are thought to be too small to warrant the investment, but the cherry picker has either lower overheads, or is using these cherries to gain a toe hold in a new market and is prepared to pay the price.

The principle that turns this strategy into a potent threat is that each cherry is a low volume but high value mini-market and is used as a stepping off point to the next, and the next, in the manner of a chain reaction.

The astute cherry picker will:

• rely on the main players not believing these segments to be attractive, and also

• take great care not to build-up any cherry into attractive propositions for the bigger players, lastly

• they do not seek fame, they never act like the market leaders.

The plan's main headings

The plan can be divided, as shown in Figure 5.9 on the following page, into eight main headings, excluding the goals. These eight headings naturally group-up into four sections.

Key Learning Point

These are:

• the marketing audit (headings 1, 2 and 3),

• the action plan (headings 4 and 5),

• the marketing programme (heading 6),

• the control mechanisms (headings 7 and 8).

The 'fruit' of the whole exercise is the 'marketing programme' (7), this is the cutting edge where the goals are realised.

Action Checklist

1. Corporate mission and goals *(i.e. the 'givens')*

2. The strategic background
Opportunities and threats from:
Political • Economic • Technical
Environmental • Social *analysis*

3. The market audit
Opportunities and threats from:
Market segmentation • Market/product life cycle
Diffusion of innovation *analysis*

4. Company and product audit
Strengths, weaknesses, assets and liabilities *analysis*
Target competitors – 'good or bad'
The competitive marketing mix
Product positioning • Company analysis

The SWOT Analysis
summarised under
heading 5.

Full details in the 'Fact
book' featured in Chapter 6.

5. Reconciliation
KSFs (key success factors) from the above SWOT • Implications from Ansoff
Product positioning issues

6. The 'grand strategy'
Specific strategy (*i.e. the game plan*) • The plan's specific mission
Marketing (S.M.A.R.T.) objectives • Sources of business i.e.target groups/segments

Tactics – to wit – **the mix:**

Classic	Extended	
Product	Process	
Price	Physical evidence	*i.e. where there is a service*
Place	People	*element to the product*
Promotion	Time based issues	
	Resources	

7. Operations: to wit – the marketing programme

8. Budgets and budget analysis

9. Control and review methods

Figure 5.9: The headings of a marketing plan

This is where the increase in market share is achieved, revenue/profit is earned, competitors are beaten etc. Everything that goes before is designed for the marketing programme to be as effective as possible. The programme will detail, action by action, who is responsible for doing what, with what objectives, with what resources and by when.

The marketing audit

Key Management Concept

This section, sometimes known as the SWOT analysis, is a continuous process. It keeps under review the total environment in which the company must establish the platform of survival which will become the launch pad to achieve its overall goals.

We examine this in some depth in Chapter 6 where we address:

1. The strategic background

Key Learning Point

This examines the total environment with which the company must deal. This is done using the checklist acronym P.L.E.E.S.T in order firstly to: identify opportunities and threats and from these to distil which of these are the 'key success factors' (KSFs.)

2. Market audit

This section again seeks to identify opportunities and threats (and those which are KSFs), this time via the examination of the total market customer base so as to enable the marketer to segment the market – (the so-called) 'target group' of 'specific customers'.

Under this heading the marketer will also analyse the various layers of lifecycle, (product market/diffusion of innovation etc.). Again so as to identify the opportunities, threats and KSFs with which the company must deal in pursuit of its goals.

3. Company and product audit

Under this heading, the marketer examines the competition in as much depth as possible. The moment a marketer identifies a customer set, s/he most probably also identifies another company who considers these customers their property, and no one else's.

This group is designed to identify the strengths and weaknesses of the main competition **AND** their assets and their liabilities (*which are not the same thing as we shall see*). Because strengths and weaknesses are relative to what the company is up against, the competition is used as the yardstick via which the marketer measures their own company.

Under this heading the marketer will examine the competitor's products and their 'positioning'. Again as a yardstick with which the marketer can measure themself.

The marketer will classify the competition as being strong or weak, bad or good. The worst situation is being confronted with a 'strong bad' competitor.

The action plan

Addressing sections 2-4 is a continuing process which produces a voluminous database of the market, too large and detailed to be included in the action plan. Thus the action plan will start with a distillation of the pertinent issues generated by the marketing audit above.

4. Reconciliation

The actual planning document which is submitted for the purposes of action and budget approval, starts here.

The document will list the KSFs succinctly and in the order in which it stimulates the strategy (heading 5 below). A key issue is the result of the Ansoff Analysis, whether the strategy to come will recommend:

- Staying with the same product, and
- staying in the same market (*market penetration*), **OR TO**
- take it into a new market (*market development*),

- Staying with the same market, and
  - develop new products (*product development*), **OR**
  - move to new markets and new products (*diversification*).

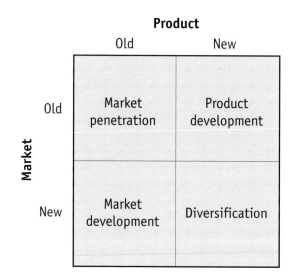

Figure 5.10: The Ansoff Analysis Grid

5. The action plan

This is in two parts:

- the grand strategy as such, and

- the tactics to be used within it.

The strategy to be adopted will be detailed as a game plan to take advantage of the KSFs which are opportunities and to defend the company against the threats prevalent in the market. It will be designed to ensure that the company can play to its strengths and assets, and to ensure that the weaknesses and liabilities of the company are:

firstly – not presented as targets for the competition, and

secondly – are addressed so that they are eventually eradicated, (but that will take time).

From here on the plan will detail the mission to be achieved. This is an aspirational statement to indicate the general direction.

It will then move on to detail the sources of business, i.e. the paying customers, often known as the target group, which are the specific market segment/s to be addressed. (*see Chapter 3 on segmentation and the decision making unit phenomenon*).

Marketing objectives

Companies frequently have corporate, company or divisional objectives which lay down the overall requirements for business performance. Such objectives are usually a fixed goal which individual parts of the organisation must try to achieve.

Marketing objectives operate at a level below this. They are strategic or tactical objectives for specific product lines, or for activities or programmes which cross over between individual products and require a concerted approach.

Examples of fairly typical marketing objectives would be:

- launch objectives for a new product line or service
- objective for improving the performance or position of an existing product or service
- objectives for a new marketing programme to improve overall range or 'system' sales.

Marketing objectives must fully define for each product or programme:

- **WHERE** the marketer wants to be and
- **WHAT** the marketer wants to achieve.

These objectives may include:

- performance elements – achieving a value of business or a particular level of market share within a fixed time

- key events or timings for a programme – e.g. 'achieve full implementation of the programme by 31 January 2002'

- key image or non-performance requirements – e.g. to raise the company's credibility or standing in a product area or with a particular target group.

Marketing objectives may be **internal** or **external** in their requirements. But they are there to state **what the plan is trying to achieve and know how it is proposed to achieve it and to act as datum against which progress can be measured**.

Guidelines for setting or assessing objectives

Be realistic

Objectives should be realistic but stretching. They should not be based on 'wishful thinking' or unrealistic assumptions, nor should they be safe and complacent.

Quantify

Performance objectives should be defined in terms of company figures, time scales and/or key deadlines.

Be consistent

If you have to set a number of objectives, make sure they are **capable of being** achieved together. Your objectives should also be consistent with high-level business or divisional objectives.

Keep the priorities clear

If there are a number of objectives, assign a priority to their achievement. Separate 'key' from 'secondary' objectives, or list the objectives in their order of priority.

At this point the plan will be specifically clear about the objectives to be achieved, these will be stated in a 'S.M.A.R.T.' format, that is to say they will be:

S pecific

M easurable

A greed

R ealistic

T ime based

The tactics whereby these objectives are achieved will consist of clear statements of policy and operation standards with respect to each element of the relevant marketing mix.

If the company is marketing solely 'goods' the classic mix will be employed. This consists of the four elements of the business known as the four 'P's'. Product, price, promotion, and place (not necessarily in that order). As we have examined in Chapter 4.

Key Management Concept

If the company is either marketing service products (such as consultancy, professional advice, training, transport, insurance, maintenance et al) **OR** is using services to add value, (include any of the above plus 'customer service'), then the classic mix must be augmented by the addition of the extended mix, consisting of the five extra elements:

Process

Services are performed, and that performance requires as much care in the design and 'production' as does the creation of a 'good', if not more so. A good is produced once, a service may be performed more than ten thousand times per day, each one by a different service provider, to a different customer, (e.g. an airline) and each of these performances must meet the required quality standard.

Physical evidence

Services are intangible – they cannot be touched, tasted, weighed, or smelled. A customer can't have a long one, short one, hot one, rough, or smooth service, (in the conventional senses of these words). So customers are continually hungry for clues as to what they have purchased – the service marketer must therefore provide some tangibility to the service – this s/he does via physical evidence which can range from the premises on which the service is performed, the work wear of those performing the service, the documentation etc.

People

It has been said that 'Service is adding people to the product' and there is a school of thought that is of the opinion that if there are not people providing the 'product' then this is not a service but a facility (*e.g. an ATM, an Automatic Telephone Reception system etc.*). This aspect, frequently known as 'customer service' will not be covered here, though it is of great importance in many markets where professional advice and consultancy are critical parts of the 'product'.

Time based issues

Time is the only objective dimension on which a service can be measured – everything else is subjective, which is an advantage in that it facilitates the possibilities of segmentation more readily than when it is a 'good' being marketed. Time comes in five flavours:

1. Punctuality
2. Duration
3. Availability

4. Speed of response

5. Speed of innovation.

Resources

Any service is highly 'capacity constrained'. The company may not sell more consultancy days than it has available, nor can the hotel sell more bed nights for tonight than it has beds tonight. The problem for any service oriented company is to ensure that at peak demand it can provide capacity, but when demand is at the bottom of the trough, it will not bleed to death through having expensive capacity lying idle. This requires a great deal of operational creativeness to arrange, and is what this aspect of the extended mix is all about.

The marketing programme

Key Learning Point

6. Operations

As discussed above (and per Figure 5.6, page 223) each element of the marketing mix is broken down into a series of interrelated Gantt Charts, detailing what gets done and when. For example the sales plan should detail when certain drives are to commence, the duration of campaigns, when exhibitions will be planned, prepared and occur etc.

Key Learning Point

The control mechanisms

7. Budgets

Budgets should be set and agreed for each of the relevant areas. The specific methods for so doing are particular to the management styles of the companies concerned. However, the principle should be that they are 'objective and task' orientated and linked closely to the realistic part of the S.M.A.R.T. objectives discussed above.

8. Control and review

No objective should be considered which is not measurable. Preferably the measurement of the attainment of objectives should be via the MIS/CIS systems of the company (*detailed in Chapter 7*).

This aspect of the marketing plan should be designed with the aim of picking up undesirable trends before they have the chance to damage the outcomes desired, and with sufficient notice for corrective action to be taken.

Building the budget

Expressing the plan in a budgeting format is an important element of shaping its implementation.

The business as a whole will have an operating budget, but what sales and marketing particularly needs to quantify are:

- how the marketer plans to achieve the required business levels – how the 'top-line' will be built up and

- what marketing or support costs will be required to achieve this.

Building the top-line (income budget)

Key Management Concept

This requires the business to be analysed into its separate area and product revenue streams, with each being targeted in terms of volume and value. The practice of illustrating these graphically, e.g. using bar charts or pie charts, assists communication. The plan should spell out the actual value or percentage change from the current year which this assumes.

To make the sales budget a working tool which can be monitored and managed, the expected business pattern should be reflected in the monthly and/or quarterly Figures as accurately as possible.

Elements of top-line budget *(See Figure 5.11 following)*

Key Management Concept

1. Existing business due to repeat

This should be the most reliable part of the whole budget, as the sales team should have fairly company information on customer's planned or scheduled requirements and are able to monitor this closely as part of their on-going relationships.

2. New business from existing customers

Again, this should be a reliable expectation to be fully included, here the deals have been evaluated and agreed for purchase before this element of the budget is set. If this business will fall part-way through a budget year and overlap into next year, this should be reflected in the Figures.

3. New business from identified customers

An area where basically the same rules apply as for element 2.

Many companies try to quantify this by using '**probability factors**' – either on whether it will arise, or when this is most likely to happen. This allows some cover and 'smoothing' of peaks and troughs.

4. New non-identified business estimate

This will be where, for example, heavy business development activity has been applied to a new segment but business has not yet reached the point of company orders from identified customers. This element could be very dynamic in business terms once it takes off, but in budgetary terms should be handled fairly conservatively until it actually happens.

5. Existing business not repeating

One of the frequent errors in building top-line budgets is to ignore this element and carry it over without thinking.

Some previous enjoyed business may now be 'out of contract'. But other elements may be 'lost' business or anticipation of possible losses, for a variety of reasons.

All the previous elements (1-4) need to be summated. But this element should be subtracted:

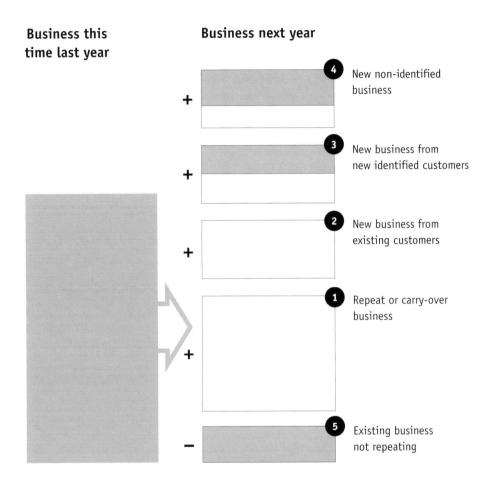

Business this time last year

Business next year

+ **4** New non-identified business

+ **3** New business from new identified customers

+ **2** New business from existing customers

+ **1** Repeat or carry-over business

− **5** Existing business not repeating

Figure 5.11: (after 'Profitable Product Management' R. Collier)

Managed cost budgets

In most companies, marketing people contribute to the development of specific areas of cost budgets where they have managerial responsibility.

This is handled to different levels of detail. Such that promotional support for the business may need splitting into:

- exhibitions
- advertising – promotion and media
- literature or other support material (*e.g. for distributors*)
- PR activities.

As with the top-line, all major areas of cost need to be planned in terms of when they will, or are likely to occur, so they can effectively be monitored. This may be on a quarterly basis (with the months of each quarter averaged out), or right down to monthly – for budget-setting.

Action Checklist

Action checklist

Review your marketing plan

Situation analysis

- Is there a sound basis for the plan from research and analysis?
- Where key information is not available, are assumptions sound?
- Is there a clear and complete picture of:
    - market/segment size and trends, including key influencing factors?
    - key competitor shares and a full competitor appraisal?

- customer segmentation, with key buyer/user needs?
- your own position (strengths, weaknesses, opportunities, threats)?

Objectives

- Does the plan clearly spell out what the marketer is trying to achieve?
- Are the objectives quantified, consistent, prioritised and S.M.A.R.T?

Strategy

- Are all viable alternatives considered?
- Are the key elements of the recommended strategy sound?
- Will the plan's strategy support overall company strategy and its key policies?
- Can the strategy be effectively implemented with available resources?
- Are all the risks fully evaluated?

Implementation

Does the 'programme':

- spell out arrangements for monitoring and control?
- detail proposals that hang together and support the strategy?
- work with the target customer groups?

The marketing audit

Deriving the foundation for a marketing strategy

Chapter 6

Synopsis

General Eisenhower is on record as saying:

> '... soon after the battle starts the original battle plan is almost useless, BUT at that point, the understanding that comes from the planning process that produced it, is invaluable.'

The main benefit from writing a marketing plan is that it forces the planner to get to know his/her battle field – the marketplace – intimately.

The following chapter examines the basic* strategic analysis that is necessary for any marketer to identify what issues must to be addressed in order to succeed, be they opportunities that can be taken advantage of, or be they threats against which the company needs to protect itself. (*i.e. the 20% of the techniques that yield 80% of the value).

It examines the four stages of analysis necessary to enable the identification of what are known as key success factors [KSF] and also to identify what competitive differential advantages may be required in the market.

It examines the macro analysis (sometimes called P.L.E.E.S.T), the micro analysis consisting of what are sometimes called porters five forces. It goes on to look at the company analysis to identify strengths and weaknesses and concludes with a brief examination of competitor analysis to identify which competitor needs to be watched carefully or may be even attacked, and which may be a good competitor, that can be tolerated.

Introduction

In 1962, a small Japanese company set out to dominate the world, by 1985 it had achieved that task, the name of the company was Komatzu and the marketplace it dominated was earth moving on major construction sites in the 'free world'. The full Komatzu story is told by Konichi Omie in his book *The Mind of the Strategist*. As far as this chapter is concerned, we'll just have a look at a few brief points.

Komatzu achieved what it did by conducting a very thorough analysis of the marketplace it wished to enter, identifying the key issues, (which Konichi Omie describes as key factors for success and we will call key success factors (KSF)) and then building a strategy around those key factors and more importantly implementing that strategy assiduously over the following twenty plus years.

We know that Komatzu set out with the deliberate intention of dominating the world market for earth moving equipment because their original strategic plan was entitled 'How we plan to murder Caterpillar'. This plan identified quite clearly that there were several factors in the marketplace that they would have to address. They identified, for example, that logistics and distribution of spare parts was a critical issue for contractors worldwide. Contractors did not buy a piece of earth moving machinery, they bought a relationship with the manufacturer and that relationship ensured that whenever their equipment required servicing, the parts were available in the shortest possible space of time, wherever that company happened to be working. The major construction projects were characteristically carried out at ends of the earth beyond normal civilisation, i.e. damming up the Nile at the Aswam Dam, or driving a major highway through the Amazon jungle.

Again Komatzu identified that it had all the skills to produce small components but knew very little about the skills required to produce components which weighed a ton or more per item. Komatzu also identified that Japan was going to be a very successful exporting country which meant that the price of the Yen would appreciate dramatically. The company also correctly anticipated that this would have the effect of putting them at a price disadvantage in the marketplace unless they could address their costs so that as the Yen appreciated, their prices outside Japan at least stayed still. Finally, they identified that the major single competitor from whom they would have to take market share if they were to succeed, was the company of Caterpillar from Peoria in the United States of America. They classified Caterpillar as potentially a very bad competitor, i.e. one that would not take any loss of its market share lightly and would retaliate as soon as it realised what was happening.

From Figure 6.1. opposite we can see the outline of the principles behind Komatzu's analysis. This is referred to as the strategic triangle. Essentially this triangle sets out that there are certain aspects of the marketplace:

- the uncontrollable environment, which we are going to examine in more detail

and

- the controllables which are the strategies necessary to address the environment and the organisation necessary to be able to implement these strategies.

The major point being that any company has to deal with the environment as it finds it and the more realistic it is about its environmental analysis then the greater the chance that the consequent strategy will work.

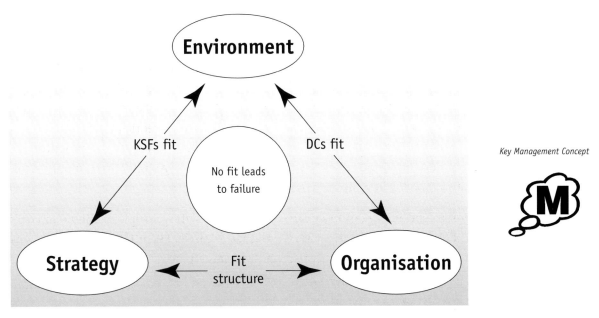

Figure 6.1: The strategic triangle

Analysis of the environment will reveal what key success factors (KSFs) must be addressed.

The strategy will also require a fit between the structure of the organisation and the strategy it intends to adopt. In the computer markets:

- large companies like IBM cannot take decisions quickly or react to events by sharp change of direction, but they do have deep pockets

- relatively small companies like Gateway don't have the muscle, range of products, or market coverage to fight a war of attrition against IBM. But they are fleet of foot and can 'turn on a sixpence'.

The ability of an organisation to handle its environment will depend on its strengths or weaknesses. In Figure 6.2 (page 258) these are shown as DCs (Distinctive competencies).

The logical order of analysis is first to examine what is known as the 'macro forces' at work, and then proceed to analyse the 'micro forces', this identifies the types and characteristics of competition to be faced. The marketer then uses this competition as a yardstick against which to evaluate their company and from this comparison starts to generate the strategies necessary to pursue the company's overall goals. This will be the order in which this chapter proceeds.

The shock of change

The law of supply and demand, and its attendant business cycle, which we examined in Chapter 1, is only one part of the modern commercial picture. Superimposed over all of that are the factors which cause the '**Shock of Change**' as per Figures 6.2, 6.3, and 6.4 following.

The whole of our environment is undergoing an alarming rapidity of change. The speed of this change is accelerating, and the rate of acceleration shows no sign of abating. Most, if not all, of the many powerful factors in the trading environment are outside the direct control of the company having to cope with them. These forces are known as the 'uncontrollables'. Just as King Canute could not reverse the tide, companies have to accept and find ways of coming to terms with these factors. To achieve its business aims the company must adapt so as to:

- take advantage of the opportunities presented, and

- ameliorate the threats posed.

Marketers must understand these forces, and the first step in that direction is to carry out the appropriate analysis. This is most frequently known as the P.E.S.T analysis:

P olitical

E conomic

S ocial

T echnical.

Alternatively this stage in the marketing planning process can be known as the S.T.E.P, or the S.P.E.T analysis, the initials stand for the same things but in one case the advocate believed that social and technical forces predominate, and in the other they believed that social and political forces are the order of the day. It is really what suits your fancy. However, as will be seen, and for reasons to be explained as we go, we will refer to it as the P.L.E.E.S.T analysis:

Action Checklist

P olitical

L egislation

E conomic

E nvironmental

S ociological

T echnical.

The marketer examines each in turn, and in combination, primarily looking for opportunities and threats in the environment and then decides which of these are key (i.e. KSFs).

Technological innovation – (The 'T' in P.L.E.E.S.T)

Key Management Concept

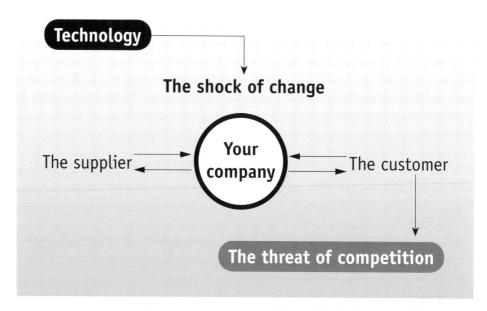

Figure 6.2: Technological innovation

Figure 6.2 above, shows the first of these factors addressed by this chapter, **Technology**. The problem with this issue is that any illustration used will rapidly date the text. But at the time of writing the two main areas of technological change which affect most markets are:

- information technology [so called IT], and

- genetic engineering.

The rate at which IT is currently changing is illustrated by such phenomena as the speed with which notebook computers and cellular telephones have rapidly became common and for many business people, indispensable items and all the indications are that they will soon be combined into one piece of kit. The promise that information technology extends for the latter part of the decade includes such innovations as personal communicators, the super-smart card, electronic shopping via the 'Internet', the intelligent house/home, video-telephones and a real time, multi-lingual, simultaneous telephone translation service. For each one of these, prototypes had already been demonstrated by the early 1990s.

The ability of genetic engineering to affect our personal and business lives is frequently less well recognised, but no less powerful than IT. Its influence ranges from:

- the adaptation of microbes to generate exotic new drugs and treatments,
- gene therapy to overcome inherited disorders, creating self-fertilising food crops,

through to:

- the 'creation' of breed-lines of animals, the organs of which can be used in human organ transplant surgery.

Again, examples of each of these already exist in the late 1990s.

Technology in all its forms, is no more than the application of science to industry, and the main engine of technology is pure science. The more pure science that is conducted, the greater the pool of knowledge from which technology can draw. The amount of pure science that can be conducted, is related to the number of scientists that are at work at any one time. The numbers of scientists in the world has grown exponentially to the point that in 1990 the International Citations Index calculated that some 93% of all scientists who have ever published, were still alive and at work in that year.

Although technology is a 'gee-whiz' generator par excellence, the P.L.E.E.S.T factor that will have the most impact on the way businesses are run is the collection of phenomena, which we lump under the heading of 'society' as per Figure 6.3.

The structure of society – (the 'S' in P.L.E.E.S.T)

Key Management Concept

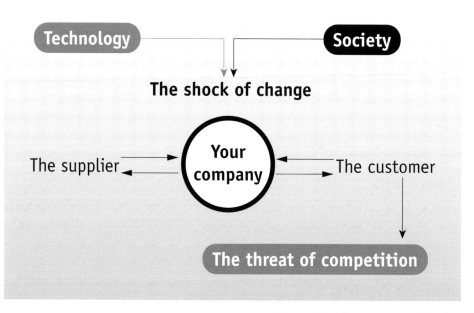

Figure 6.3: The structure of society

The structure of 'society' is changing as are the attitudes contained. These are the cornerstones of culture, and throughout the world, all be it at differing rates, cultures are changing more rapidly than at any other time in human history. People will no longer have to go abroad to suffer 'culture shock', its happening all around them.

To illustrate how the structure of society is changing, just examine some current issues from within the United Kingdom.

Demographics

The normal family?

The proportion of single parent households, which represented only one in thirteen family households in 1970, had risen to one in five in 1999. This group represents a huge and rising portion of society, and in the sense that it is the most frequently occurring single form, it now represents the UK norm.

Family size

The average number of children per family in the early 70s was 2.4. It is now said to be some 1.4 and falling. This is what has been called the 'demographic dip'. Many sections of the UK population are not replacing themselves.

Single people

With some six million single person households, the United Kingdom has the largest proportion of its adult population living on their own, of any country within the European Community.

An ageing population

Due to the demographic dip, and the way people are living longer healthier lives, the UK population is ageing rapidly, such that by the year 2000 more than 50% of the population will be over fifty years of age.

These changes in our age profile are also affecting the distribution of wealth in society, as more insurance policies pay out and mortgages mature and/or large houses get exchanged for smaller bungalows or flats for retirement.

Implications

The demographic dip heralds two real problems for any company in either the service sector or using service to add value:

- For a people industry: where are tomorrow's employees to come from?

and

- How are tomorrow's customers going to behave, their lifestyles will be so different from anything known before?

  [Marketers must be in a position to address lifestyle issues, it plays an increasingly central role in consumer marketing.]

The speed and direction of changing lifestyles, and the way these effect business (*and will continue to*) has been provocatively brought to the attention of many people by Faith Popcorn in her book *The Popcorn Report* published in the early 90s.

The changing attitudes of society

Lifestyles are an expression of people's attitudes, their belief systems, opinions and understanding of the world in which they live. These are also changing dramatically.

A change of particular note is the increasing awareness of, and active concern about, the environment.

This 'E' is for Environment (and/or Ecology) and, is the second E of the P.L.E.E.S.T analysis (*the first being the 'E' of Economy*).

Ecology/environment

Some companies have cynically tried to ride the crest of this wave under false pretences, and when found out, the customer's reactions have often destroyed the business.

Other companies have genuinely adapted their operations and their offerings to the market, and have enjoyed considerable extra revenue as a result.

Image

The 'social image' of a company or its country of origin is becoming an increasingly important influence on customer behaviour. For example:

- when Nestle were heavily criticised for their marketing of 'Baby Formula milk feed' which caused such trauma in West Africa, or

- when Exxon International's oil tanker the Exxon Valdez, polluted Prince William Sound in Alaska.

The social image of a country of origin can also have a 'halo effect' on the company. For example Japan has positive images of quality and technology, but its association with whaling, the death of dolphins when tuna fishing, and the fact that its markets are effectively closed to the rest of the world, are also powerful negative factors.

Attitudes toward price

There is also a gathering body of evidence to indicate that the prolonged recession of the 80s and 90s has fundamentally changed the way people shop with respect to price. To quote a 1995 MRS conference paper:

> '…the indications from many current studies are that customers are moving from their former attitude that price could be a positive indicator of quality, through a situation of imposed price sensitivity caused by the current recession, towards a re-evaluation which leads to 'internalised price sensitivity'. This can be thought of as a concern about cost per se, value trade offs, and **changed** importance weights associated with price and quality.
>
> This heralds a much longer healing process, which many believe will never fully materialise even when the recession is fully over.

The slow pattern of consumer spending in 1999 shows how true this is.

Political issues = government and legislation

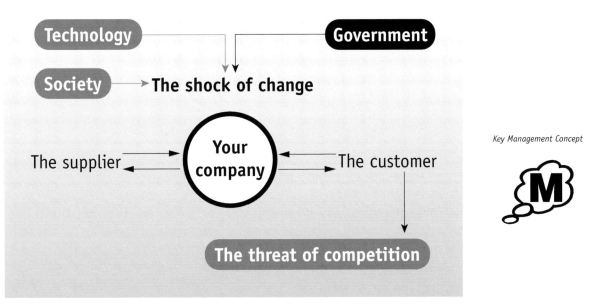

Figure 6.4: Government – a major engine of change

Key Management Concept

Economics

Figure 6.4 above shows that government, (*and the legislation produced, the 'L' in P.L.E.E.S.T*) is a major engine of change. The most immediately notable effect of government is how well (*or otherwise*) they are acting as custodians of their country's economy.

Political stability

The second element of government, the 'P' in P.L.E.E.S.T, is to do with political stability. Whether companies are dealing with home or export markets, their political stability is a major cause for concern.

In this respect, governments have been called 'the major source of uncertainty in this century' and perhaps the next.

Both at home and abroad the governance of many of the nations with which we wish to do business, seem unable to handle change peacefully. Some commentators have observed that if we in Europe fail to get our act together, the resulting political chaos will make the troubles and massacres in the Congo for example, and the suppression of Chechinia look like a vicar's tea party.

However, these are the extreme issues, but there are no less important issues closer to home which will have a profound impact on the way that business can be conducted.

Legislation

Although legislation (the 'L' in P.L.E.E.S.T) affects us all, some business sectors are affected more than most in terms of the extent that 'compliance' will constrain their freedom to manoeuvre in the marketplace. Marketing within the financial service sector being perhaps the most regulated. Although this is frequently the operational concern of the 'compliance' department within these companies, the marketer of financial services must address these issues earlier in the marketing process than most. Because so many companies are now using 'financial products' to help fund their clients – in both business to business and consumer markets – what constrains the financial services sector affects all markets.

The uncertainties of the political infrastructures generating and influencing the application of this legislation can make the process a nightmare.

The implications of cycles and change

The evidence suggests that each and every element of the commercial environment represented within the P.L.E.E.S.T acronym will continue to change rapidly (*but each at a different rate*) for the foreseeable future.

In this sea of change, the only island of certainty is the customer, the logical implication of the saying 'no customer, no business', is that if the company has customers, it will survive at the very least, and given the right wind will also thrive.

The marketing concept, with its emphasis on focusing the business on the needs of the customer, is therefore the only management philosophy capable of handling the swings and arrows of not only the outrageous 'supply and demand' cycle, but also the inherent instabilities in the P.L.E.E.S.T related issues today.

Format for recording the macro analysis

In Figure 6.5 overleaf we can see the layout of the sort of form that marketing analysts will use in order to distil and record the main elements of their work. We see down the left hand column under 'issues', the P.L.E.E.S.T analysis and in the centre column we see the 'relevance'. It is important here to identify whether or not the factors are opportunities or threats and clearly identify them as such. Finally in the right hand column, we see some suggested response. The degree to which this response becomes important depends on whether the factor identified is a key success factor (KSF) or not.

Issue	Relevance i.e. O or T?	A KSF? – Response?
Political		
Legislation		
Economic		
Environment		
Social		
Demographic		
Technical		

Action Checklist

Figure 6.5: Analysing segment macro environments

Key Learning Point

A key success factor can either be an opportunity or a threat. As an 'opportunity' – the company can thrive if it takes advantage. As a 'threat' – the company will fail if it does not raise its guard.

When completing the proforma as per Figure 6.5 above, it is as well to remember that there can be more than one issue per category. For example take 'political'. There could be a change of government in the United Kingdom, the manifesto of which could pose threats for some companies, and opportunities for others. Whilst at the same time, there could be a change of commissioners in Europe, with outcomes that could pose different opportunities and threats.

It is also possible for one factor to spread across several topic boxes. For example, in the late 90s Labour responded to British Telecoms' complaints that it was unfairly being prevented from competing with the new cable companies. In addition to TV entertainment, they could offer telephone, fax and Internet connections, whereas BT was not allowed to offer TV.

Labour wanted to make education a major plank in its manifesto, and that meant using IT to the full extent for that process. The most practical solution for 'putting a PC on every child's desk was what was known as the 'thin client' strategy i.e. the PC on the child's desk is only an intelligent terminal, data and programmes are run from a central server in the area which is also serving a number of other schools. This required the schools to be connected via ISDN enabling the thin client strategy, via allowing the fastest access to the world wide web as well. However, few schools were connected to ISDN lines. So, Labour and BT struck a well publicised deal, which stipulated that when in government, Labour would allow BT to compete with the cable companies in return for connecting all schools in the UK to ISDN free.

Now, if the company is in either education, or IT software or hardware, then this factor would have appeared under politics, legislation, social, and technical, and in each it could be either a threat, or an opportunity, depending on which sector of the market the company served.

Finally, it could be that there are no relevant issues under a particular topic for your company, if that is genuinely the case so be it, don't try and force anything to fit just because there is an empty box. However, before abandoning that empty box, do check with a colleague that they agree, and that there is not something that has been overlooked. This is a useful practice anyway, empty box or not.

Key Learning Point

Activity

Activity No. 8

Take the marketplace for the product that was identified in the exercises of Chapter 2 and conduct a macro (P.L.E.E.S.T) analysis using the format as per the proforma below.

Issue	Relevance i.e. O or T?	A KSF? – Response?
Political		
Legislation		
Economic		
Environment		
Social		
Demographic		
Technical		

Identifying the competition

Figure 6.6 overleaf sets out the central thinking suggested by Professor Michael Porter of Harvard, these issues are often referred to as Porter's Five Forces. This micro analysis looks at what sort of competition a company will face in pursuit of its goals.

We have seen the power struggle that exists between suppliers and customers as they struggle over the share of market profits which each desires to obtain. This battle also includes current competitors and these fall into two basic categories: direct and indirect. We all know who our direct competitors are, these are companies in the marketplace which supply the same goods or services as we do, at least generically. They will offer (*approximately*) the same bundles of benefits to the marketplace.

Direct competitors are the enemy you can see. However, there is often as much if not more danger from those competitors you can't see, the indirect competitors. To understand the idea of the indirect competitor one has to realise that all vendors are competing for their customer's finite resources. These resources may be 'time', but are more likely to be money. So whatever the customer, be it a business or a consumer, if they have spent that money elsewhere they are unable to spend it with your company. What a company spends on redesigning its logo (*£1+ million in the case of British Petroleum*) or what it spends on research and development (*£9 billion per annum in the case of IBM*) it may not spend, for example, on health care for its workers, or an advertising campaign. What a consumer spends on renovating their home, or refurnishing their lounge, they may not spend on their holiday. Thus a marketer should always be looking to find out what customers consider to be alternative viable uses of their scarce resource.

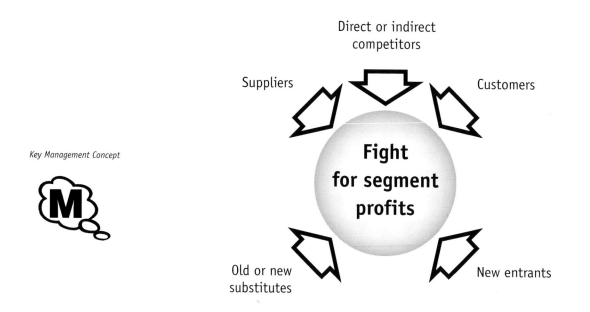

Key Management Concept

Figure 6.6: Micro analysis

Substitutes are different from indirect competition. They are other ways of deriving the same or similar benefits to the ones offered by your goods or service. Examples of substitutes would be e-mails or faxes as opposed to conventional letter post for the postal service of any given country. Another example of new or potential substitutes might well be (*as identified by the major airlines in the world*) video conferencing as a replacement for holding management meetings. This will result in fewer business class travellers circling the globe because nearly all but the most critical business meetings would be carried out talking to other members of that meeting via a PC screen.

New entrants to a market are companies who are not currently competing in that marketplace but who have the ability to enter that marketplace providing there are no barriers in place. For example there is Richard Branson's Virgin organisation, competing now in the cosmetics market directly against Body Shop.

In summary, Figure 6.6 is a checklist used by the marketer to identify the type of competition they will face and from where.

Figure 6.7 sets out the format for recording this analysis and again it will identify opportunities and threats and whether or not these are key success factors. The marketer proceeds, via the macro and the micro analysis above, to evaluate how able the company is to take advantage of the opportunities and defend itself against the potential degradations of the threats.

Issue	Relevance i.e. O or T?	A KSF? – Response?
Buyers		
Direct competitors		
New entrants		
New substitutes		
Suppliers		
Indirect competitors		

Action Checklist

Figure 6.7: Analysing segment structural forces

Figure 6.8 illustrates the rationale for the process. The left hand branch of the process (*macro and micro analysis*) establishes the key success factors (Os and Ts) which must be addressed. Against this the right hand branch establishes the tools (strengths or weaknesses*) which are available to the company (**here termed distinctive competencies or DCs*). In order to survive and thrive some constructive way must be found to match the right hand branch with the left. This will be via generating a range of strategies and possible competitive differentials, from which the most suitable will be selected.

Key Management Concept

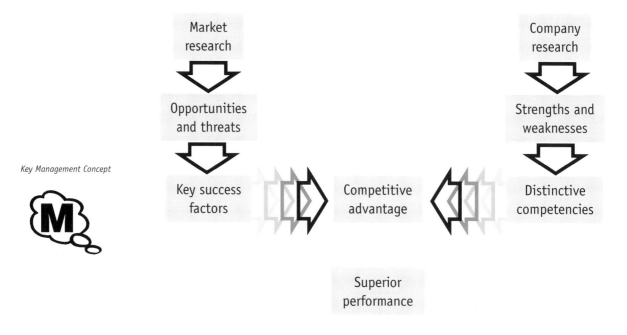

Figure 6.8: Rationale for SWOT analysis

As mentioned earlier perhaps the largest single source of threat is competition – this may be direct or indirect. Or the market may be starting to move over to a substitute product (*i.e. at the end of its life cycle*). The mobile phone taking over from the fixed line telephone, or domestic airlines taking over from railways and bus services are both examples of direct substitutions.

The sequence in which the analysis of strengths and weaknesses is conducted, is firstly to evaluate the competition and use that evaluation as the yardstick against which to gauge the strengths and weaknesses of one's own organisation. The formats of the analysis employed for both one's own company, and that of the competition are identical, i.e. in order to be able to compare like with like, the same framework must be employed.

This process involves re-visiting Michael Porter as can be seen in Figure 6.9 below, this time entitled 'Porter's five factors'.

Key Management Concept

Figure 6.9: Porter's five competency factors analysing strengths and weaknesses

Porter identifies five essential business disciplines that enable a company to compete. Moving clockwise from purchasing and supply we see that the ability to access the supply of labour, materials, other factors like electricity, water, consumables and so forth, at a reasonable cost of both time and effort, is an important starting point for any organisation.

Previously, companies would locate next to their sources of energy, so we see the steel industry setting up in Sheffield near the Yorkshire coal fields, or millers setting up on the river bank to power their water wheel driven grindstones. In the age of industries based on intellectual property, software companies are moving to places like Bangalor in Southern India to be able to access the huge pool of relatively cheap talent writing software.

The second issue is to be able to add value. If we are a producer of goods, we must know how competent we are at the production process. Can we develop particular processes which are unique to ourselves such as the Pilkingtons' float glass process which has given Pilkingtons the cost edge over any producer of window glass in the world. If we are a service company, we add value via the operation of our service delivery process and again a great source of competitive advantage can be thus obtained as is illustrated by Federal Express.

In order to generate income, we have to be able to sell our goods or service to the marketplace. How good are we at doing that? (*In sections below we will examine the company's sales and marketing competencies in more detail.*)

The next area is about moving things around. Even in the service sector, in order to be able to perform our service to the optimum there are logistical problems to overcome, both of people and of material.

If we are producing goods, it stands to reason that getting those goods to the marketplace is a critical factor in our ability to compete. Nowadays the discipline of logistics is recognised as being a competency in its own right, e.g. Lanes Transport's relationship with Body Shop.

So far we have examined the means by which revenue is generated. How the company manages that revenue, accesses finance for investment (and indeed their cost of capital) can be likened to the cement that holds the other four bricks into the wall. This last factor examines how well the company manages its cash flow and sells itself to the sources of capital such as share holders, banks and other institutions.

Analysing sales and marketing competency

We can see in checklists 6a to 6d, for the purposes of analysis, the marketer can break down the sales and marketing operation into four major headings:

Action Checklist

- Marketing performance
- Strategic variables
- Marketing mix effectiveness
- Marketing organisation.

Checklist 6a – marketing performance

Assessed per product, customer and/or region

Action Checklist

- Customer satisfaction
- Sales (vol/val)
- Market share
- Revenue
- Costs
- Cash flows
- Margins
- ROI.

i) Current market performance examines:

- The strategic variables employed
- How effective the marketing mix is, and
- How well organised the company is to be effective.

Assessing marketing performance requires the examination for example, of:

- who the customers are
- what the competitive differential is for that particular company
- what market share the company has been able to obtain
- what the trends in that market share are. Is it on the increase, is it static or on the decrease?

All sorts of revenues and costs are involved in marketing operations, so how well does the company manage its cash flow? The bottom line of course is return on investment.

Checklist 6b – strategic variables

- Marketing objectives
- Market choices
- DCs
- Competitive positioning
- Portfolio balance.

ii) Strategic variables

Key Management Concept

It is important to be able to understand what the competitors are trying to achieve, i.e. what their marketing objectives are. Sometimes they state these quite clearly in their company returns and in their releases. Sometimes the analyst has to infer what their objectives are from their actions.

It is also important to understand whether the company has chosen to address its specific markets deliberately or whether it is just an accident. Whichever way the market was chosen the most important thing is how healthy is that market, what is actually happening to the 'food chain' within that marketplace and where-abouts is that market on its product life cycle.

If the company is a large organisation, does it have a portfolio of markets each at a different stage of the life cycle, so that as one market fades away others are coming to fruition? And is there the seed corn of future markets being developed?

In each of these markets we need to know how competitive the company is, what its strategic competencies are, and what are its competitive differentials. In others we need to know how well positioned the company is within its various marketplaces.

In addition to having a portfolio of markets, it is also important that the company should have a portfolio of products. In other words:

- those products that are producing cash at the moment
- those that will produce cash in the future
- those that are being used to dominate the market
- those which have done all that and are on their way out.

A healthy business is one with a healthy portfolio of markets and products so as to ensure continuity and that not all its eggs are in any one basket.

Checklist 6c – marketing mix effectiveness

- Products

- Services, prices and financial terms

- Promotion

- Distribution

- Operational efficiency.

iii) Marketing mix effectiveness

When assessing the marketing mix effectiveness of an organisation, in addition to products (*be they goods or services*) an evaluation should be conducted of how suited are the pricing strategies to the marketplace, and (*particularly in business to business*) what sort of funding strategy is used to enable the customer to buy.

The marketing mix precedes, in its classic format, to look at promotion, advertising, public relations, exhibitions, direct mail and so forth.

As we have seen in Chapter 4, 'distribution' is more than just 'transport' and 'logistics', it is concerned with the channels in the market used to reach the customer. Are these agents, distributors, wholesalers etc? Are we in an industry that requires business partners, in other words, people who add value to the product before selling it on (value added resellers – VARs)?

Finally, when assessing the marketing mix effectiveness, it is important to know the commercial equivalent of the order of battle. How well is the company organised to be able to pursue its markets, and if this company is a competitor, how well are they able to respond to a competitive threat? How good do we believe their marketing information systems to be, including market research and customer information systems? And are these making a direct input into the planning and control system processes? How closely coupled is the marketing organisation with the production and delivery systems of the company? In other words can it deliver what it sells?

Is marketing a philosophy adopted by everyone throughout the organisation or is it considered to be a function of a small elite department somewhere close to the board and of no concern to anybody else? The more that marketing is a company philosophy the more able the marketing company is to carry the rest of the company with it when taking an initiative.

Checklist 6d – marketing organisation

- Marketing information
- Planning and control system
- Production and delivery processes
- Functional integration
- Marketing skills and training
- Marketing orientation.

iv) Marketing organisation

Finally, what about the skills and training of that organisation, what are its levels of skills and what programmes are in place to improve those skills and to maintain them as people move through their careers and/or leave the company for other employers?

Figure 6.10 overleaf shows the analysis checklist for the whole of the above.

Factor	Strength	Weakness	Our response
Purchase and supply			
Production and operation			
Transport and logistics			
Financial management			
Sales and marketing	As below		
Market performance			
Strategic variables			
Mix effectiveness			
Marketing origin			

Figure 6.10: Company analysis checklist for strengths and weaknesses

Action Checklist

Marketing assets and liabilities

Key Management Concept

In the previous section we looked at strengths and weaknesses. These are either the presence or the absence of skills within the company (*or alternatively the ability to access those necessary skills that happen to be outside the company*), for example, the ability to either do one's own advertising, one's own market research or the ability to hire and employ advertising, marketing, research or design agencies to do such things on the company's behalf. What is often confused with strengths and weaknesses are assets and liabilities. The difference between the two quite simply lies within the answer to the question, 'can the company do it again?'

To illustrate: a company may well have a very large brand share, however, that brand share is the fruit of somebody's skill in the past, that person or persons could have left. Even though that originator has gone, the brand share remains to generate revenue for the company. But if the company were to try and enter new markets, because that skill is no longer present, it may not be able to be as successful as previously. The brand share is therefore an asset and the skill to build it was a strength but the lack of that skill is now a weakness.

Figures 6.11a, b and c and Figure 6.12 set out the various stages of analysis for assets and liabilities. These fall under three major headings:

- Customer based assets
- Distribution based assets
- Internally based assets.

In 6.11a we see assets in terms of customers. It is clear that for any company, customers are a very valuable asset indeed. Some people would argue that customers are the only assets of the company. One way or another it is important for the company to understand how best to address customers' needs.

How well does the quality that the company offers, (by way of specification say) fit in with these needs. Does the company understand by what criteria the customer actually assesses quality?

In terms of a competitive differential, does the company offer products, (be they goods or services), which are superior to the competition? In terms of service, (be that customer service, or a service which is part of the product such as installation, maintenance, training and so forth), does this meet and hopefully exceed customers' expectations?

'**Superior pricing**' is not about being cheaper or being more expensive, but that the pricing strategy chosen is the one that is the most appropriate to the marketplace (*for pricing strategies see Chapter 4, part II*).

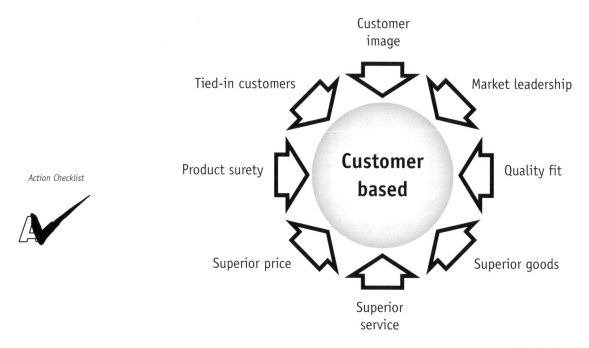

Action Checklist

Figure 6.11a: Marketing assests

In the above:

'**Product surety**' asks what sort of guarantees and warranties exist to help calm customer anxieties.

'**Tied-in customers**' refers to those customers who either are contracted, or for other reasons are unlikely to go elsewhere. The larger the tied-in base the more secure is a company.

And finally, overall does the company enjoy a superior image to its competitors in the market? It is interesting that everything else can be relatively poor, but if the image is good, it will carry the company through. An example is Marks & Spencer, although cracks have already appeared in much of Marks & Spencers' infrastructure, it is still able to command a premium price for its goods.

Knowing the quality of a company's customers is one thing, knowing how well the company is able to get its goods or services to those customers is another.

And here we address Figure 6.11b. which examines the distribution base of the company. This involves transportation and logistics but more importantly refers to routes to market. Starting at the top:

'**Broad coverage**' – what proportion of the market does it cover in terms of numbers and types of customers? An example of this would be a mobile telephone operator, such as Orange, held back for many years by not being able to cover the whole country as well as Vodafone or Cellnet, but worse off still was Mercury with its One2One mainly covering the South East and even then only really being useful within a 50 mile radius of the centre of London.

Does the company employ the best dealers in its marketplace? This is of particular importance if a company is in high technology and has to employ value added resellers. No matter how excellent the goods or service, if that final link in the chain is faulty, the company will not achieve its full potential.

'**Forward integration**' and '**forward linkages**' are to do with how far down the chain of distribution, towards the origins of the food chain, is the company able to influence what goes on. Integration is where the company actually owns some or all of its routes to market. A good example of this is that most of the shoe retail shops in the United Kingdom are owned by the Allied British Shoe Manufacturers.

'**Unique methods**' asks if the company is able to gain a strategic advantage via using unique distribution methods. We see this illustrated in the case of DELL Computers. Michael Dell innovated selling personal computers direct from the factory whilst the rest of the market was convinced that the only way to reach the customer was via high street retailers. This is not the only reason for DELL's success, i.e. increasingly DELL's direct marketing is integrated with 'built to demand'.

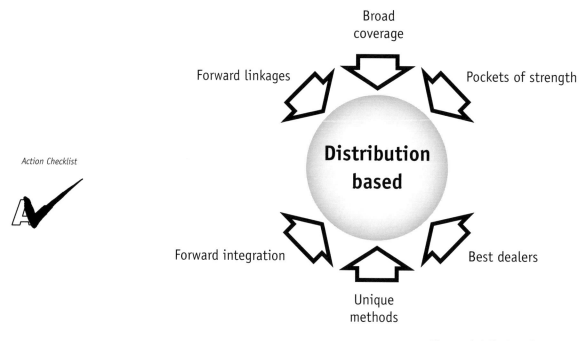

Action Checklist

Figure 6.11b: Marketing assests

Just as in checklist 6.b, Figure 6.11c looks internally at the company's ability to conduct its marketing. How competent is management and the workforce and how committed are they to the marketing culture that the company must adopt in order to be able to compete in today's marketplaces?

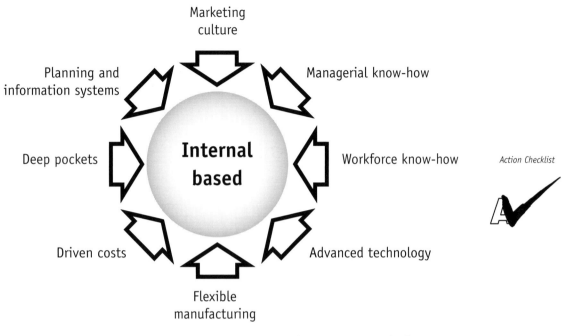

Action Checklist

Figure 6.11c: Marketing assests

Two other factors stand out for particular mention in Figure 6.11c. Firstly, '**flexible manufacturing**' which, allied with '**advanced technology**', will enable the company to stay abreast of any twist and turns in the market, and with any acceleration in the rate of technological advance.

Secondly, '**deep pockets**'. In the event of a competitive war of any sort, the question is how big is the 'war chest'. Only IBM could have made the largest single loss in commercial history (circa $35billion). We currently see that Microsoft has generated a $200billion war chest to be able to fight off the depredations that may occur as a result of the examination of its business by the United States Department of Justice. The presence of a war chest may well deter competitive action, opponents will be able to see that such a resource will enable the competitor to endure more pain for longer than they can.

Type	Assets	Liabilities	Action
Customer based			
Distribution based			
Internally based			

Action Checklist

Figure 6.12: A marketing assets and liabilities audit matrix

Finally, we see in Figure 6.12 a format for the reconciliation of the analysis of a companys' assets or liabilities. The reader is reminded that this analysis (as per checklist 6a-b, and Figures 6.11 and 6.12) is firstly carried out for the competitor, and then it is used as a yardstick against which to measure the strengths, weaknesses, assets and liabilities of one's own company.

Activity No. 9

In Chapters 2 and 4 we identified a major competitor as a datum against which we could measure our products. Firstly: take the same competitor and apply the analysis we have just discussed to them, using the two proforma following:

A competitor's company analysis checklist

For strengths and weaknesses

Factor	Strength	Weakness	Our response
Purchase and supply			
Production and operation			
Transport and logistics			
Financial management			
Sales and marketing	**As below**		
Market performance			
Strategic variables			
Mix effectiveness			
Marketing origin			

A competitor's marketing assets and liabilities audit matrix

Action Checklist

Type	Assets	Liabilities	Action
Customer based			
Distribution based			
Internally based			

Activity No. 10

Activity

Now we need to see what disparities exist between us and the competition. Using the previous two analysis of the competitor as a datum, assess how your company stands re. its strengths and weaknesses compared to theirs.

Our company analysis checklist

Strengths and weaknesses v/s the competition

Factor	Strength	Weakness	Our response
Purchase and supply			
Production and operation			
Transport and logistics			
Financial management			
Sales and marketing	As below		
Market performance			
Strategic variables			
Mix effectiveness			
Marketing origin			

Action Checklist

Our assets and liabilities audit matrix

Type	Assets	Liabilities	Action
Customer based			
Distribution based			
Internally based			

Action Checklist

Specific to the competition

By comparing how you stand to your main competition both in strengths and assets, yours versus theirs, and weaknesses and liabilities, again compared to theirs, a suggestion of either how we may be able to beat them OR how they may be able to beat our company, is starting to emerge.

Now, if your company does have the edge, we need to be able to see whether we should take the initiative and attack, or whether it would be best to leave them alone.

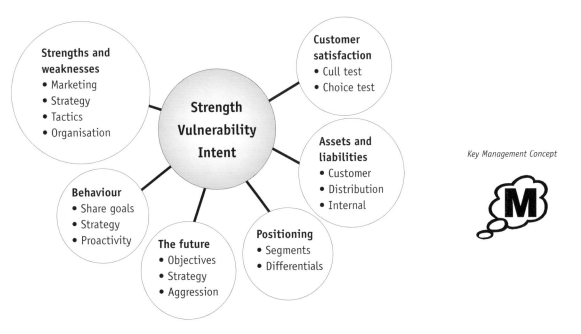

Key Management Concept

Figure 6.13: Assessing a competitor

Figure 6.13 sets out the six areas under which the competitor should be analysed, and as the reader will observe, this is a summary of all the foregoing analysis of strengths, weaknesses, assets and liabilities. The final issue is to determine whether or not we can consider each of the direct competitors as being good or bad.

In Figure 6.14 shown below, the label 'bad' for a competitor suggests that they should be watched assiduously and not trusted an inch, and at the earliest opportunity attacked i.e. the company decides to get its retaliation in first, a sort of commercial Pearl Harbour.

Key Management Concept

Characteristics	Are they 'good'	Or are they 'bad'
Objective	Realistic	Ambitious
Strategy	Logical	Unpredicatable
Share fighting	On benefits	On price
Capacity	Realistic	Optimistic
Targeting	Focused	Broad scope
Offerings	Differential	'Me too'

Figure 6.14: 'Good' and 'bad' competitors

The label 'good' indicates that although we will tolerate that competitor, we should not trust them, and we still keep them under surveillance. Even the most friendly of nations maintain an intelligence facility against its allies.

A good competitor is allowed to exist sometimes for fear of what may come after. The competitor is seen as being similar to the stopper on a bottle, the removal of which could open a Pandora's Box (*to mix the metaphor*), the like of which is unknown and therefore to be feared. The rule being, the better the competitor you know, than the one you don't.

The characteristics against which we compare whether companies are good or bad are as follows:

The objectives

Are these reasonable and realistic? If so – okay, but if they appear to be over ambitious, beware.

Strategy

How predictable is the strategy of the competitor? Surprise can provide a competitor with a major advantage.

Share fighting

A competitor pursuing market share on the basis of price, can start a price war which will have detrimental effect on everyone in the marketplace.

Capacity

This 'capacity' includes not only a company's production capacity but also its financial resources. Capacity in excess of requirements vis-à-vis its current market can indicate whether or not the company should be watched more closely. Over capacity means that the company will either have to return those resources to its shareholders or find some way of employing them to advantage, so as to yield the necessary return on capital that the financial markets require.

Targeting

In most cases a competitor focusing on a niche clearly identifies its wish to be left alone. *'This is my neck of the woods and these are my customers, if you don't rattle my cage, I won't rattle yours.'* However, the same company could be employing a strategy of rolling segmentation via 'cherry picking' (*moving from one bridgehead to the next*), and could provide its competitors with a severe headache.

The offering

Anything that purports to be selling something identical to yours must be watched closely. They provide a real and present danger to the survival of your company in its marketplace.

Activity No. 11

Finally, do the exercise on the following proforma based on Figure 6.14 (page 294) to classify whether this competitor is 'bad' and therefore your company should try to put them out of your market, or they are 'good' and you should tolerate, if not actually collaborate with them.

'Good' and 'bad' competitors

Characteristics	Are they 'good'	Or are they 'bad'
Objective	Realistic	Ambitious
Strategy	Logical	Unpredicatable
Share fighting	On benefits	On price
Capacity	Realistic	Optimistic
Targeting	Focused	Broad scope
Offerings	Differential	'Me too'

In summary

The above chapter is the present day equivalent of the tools used by Komatzu for the analysis which was conducted from 1962 to 1965 to generate the strategy which enabled it to dominate the world market for earth moving plant by 1985.

Komatzu identified its key factors for success. The first of these KSFs mentioned was the ability to distribute spare parts and to service contractors operating on construction sites throughout the free world. The plan Komatzu used to gain this skill was to become a Caterpillar distributor in China and Formosa (as it was then called), this brought it very close to Caterpillar and Komatzu was thus able to learn about the skills it required and also the adversary that eventually it would have to fight.

The key success factor of being able to manufacture components on a very large scale, (i.e. when weighing a ton or so), was addressed by helping Caterpillar to sub-contract the manufacture of these components to low labour cost areas such as Formosa and other South East Asian countries.

The task of keeping the costs of manufacture continually reducing so that, with an appreciating Yen, at least its prices to the end customers were enabled to stand still in real terms, was achieved by adopting and in fact even developing the concept of Kaizen which as the reader will know from Chapter 1, is a strategy of continually producing 1% improvement all round. This approach it kept to itself and did not share with Caterpillar.

Using these, amongst many other factors, Komatzu was able to position itself, over the twenty years (1965 to 1985), so that when in 1985 a technology war broke out between John Deer, Ford and Caterpillar, Komatzu was able to take advantage of the confusion and divide and rule the market, so that when the dust cleared they were in command of the high ground. Komatzu had the strategic long-term vision which typifies the mind of the real business strategist today.

Getting the feedback

Chapter 7

Synopsis

Successful marketing critically depends on building relationships, thus the listening part of the communication process is absolutely vital. As Tom Peter's said:

> *'listening IS part of the product'*.

Additionally it is important to realise that market (or marketing) research is only one part of the overall market information system via which the marketer listens to the customers and their influencers. In this chapter we are going to concentrate on just two parts of the information mix, that is the marketing intelligence system, and market or marketing research.

Introduction

There is a recognised difference between market and marketing research. The former is similar to a balance sheet in that it provides a 'snapshot in time', it paints a picture of what the market dimensions were when that 'Polaroid' was taken. The latter (marketing research), goes further and provides the marketeer with the ability to make marketing decisions as to future actions, strategies, policies and plans.

Marketing research addresses the questions such as:

- *Why does the market behave in this way?*

or

- *What would happen if this or that action were to be taken?*

But before we examine the various tools, it would be useful to define the different categories of information.

Types of information

There are essentially four categories of information, they fall into a two-by-two matrix as follows:

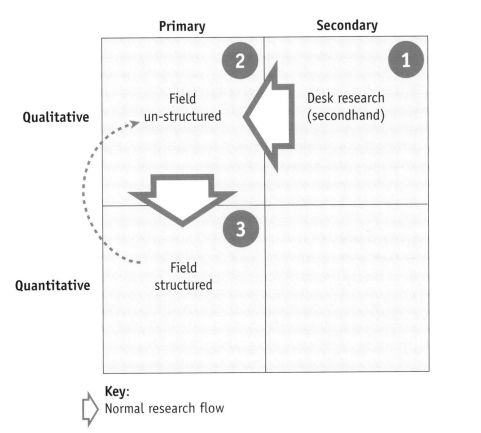

Key Management Concept

Figure 7.1: The information matrix

Secondary data via desk research

There are a plethora of secondary data sources. If coming to the topic de novo the researcher will start wide, and explore what has already been published on this topic. Secondary data is said to be obtained via desk research, although the library connotations have almost faded into obscurity in favour of 'on-line' host databases such as Night Rider and the Internet. Thus the research is still conducted at a 'desk'. Other on-line sources are 'Infomat', part of the Dun & Bradstreet empire and Reuters. These databases are what is known as 'host databases' in that they provide a 'one point of entry' access to the data which may be produced, and sometimes still held by the organisations originating the data, such as the *Financial Times*, or Dow Jones.

There are also a wide range of on-line sources which can be accessed direct, such as Predicast, Target Group Index [TGI], Mintel, and the *Financial Times* etc.

The major benefit of on-line data is that it can be accessed at a very modest cost compared to the cost of primary research, another is the speed with which the data can be obtained. However, direct access to a 'host' database is usually restricted to people or companies who are members, i.e. they have an existing account, and can be billed for the time used and the per-page cost of the data accessed.

Throughout the world there are many bureaux providers of secondary data search, amongst other services, these provide indirect access to on-line databases both host and otherwise. Amongst these is The Chartered Institute of Marketing (CIM) to which runs a service called 'INFOMARK', this provides indirect access on-line and other secondary data. This service is open to CIM members and non-members alike (though members pay less).

Governments throughout the world are major sources of secondary information, some better than the United Kingdom, (where there is no Freedom of Information Act), but many far less organised and fruitful. Several major countries also publish guides to what previous research is for sale, as in the UK.

Secondary data will be used to bring the researcher up-to-speed with the main issues in the market, and to identify those areas where information gaps exist. These gaps, if material to the objectives of the research, will now need to be filled via primary research.

However, it is dangerous to accept any secondary data at its face value. The researcher should never forget that it is 'secondhand', i.e. obtained by someone else, at some other time, for some other purpose than the researcher's objectives. It should therefore always be tested for impartiality, validity, and reliability. In this context these are taken as meaning:

Key Question

Impartiality

'Partial data' is produced when there is a 'hidden agenda' to the research. Often research is carried out to 'prove a point', or the data has been edited with such a motive. Trade associations, and industry groups are notorious for so slanting the data they present to the outside world. The 'sharp' researcher must ensure that he/she is satisfied that whatever bias exists, (some bias will always be present) it does not put his/her research objectives in jeopardy.

Validity

That is to say that the research measures what it purports to measure. A notable example to illustrate is the 'Hawthorn Studies' where the initial research was to measure assembly shop productivity as a function of working conditions. The hypothesis being that 'the better the conditions, the higher the workforce productivity'. A specific variable under investigation was lighting as an aspect of working conditions. Better lighting did seem to result in higher productivity, but when the quality of lighting was reduced, productivity did not decline apace. Later research was able to show that assembly shop workers were responding to heightened levels of management attention, they had never seen managers on the shop floor before, let alone so many.

Reliability

Key Question

This topic asks whether the research methodology is up to the job? A simple test is: would the marketer be satisfied with the way this research were carried out if he/she were to commission it, and to pay out of their own budget?

Primary information via 'field research'

Primary research is conducted to fill information gaps that the secondary data has not been able to satisfy. Primary data can be obtained via a matrix of research approaches.

Key Management Concept

AD-HOC vs. **MULTI-CLIENT** on the one axis, and

QUALITATIVE vs. **QUANTITATIVE** on the other.

Ad hoc studies

The research can be commissioned direct by the marketer, to be conducted on his/her behalf, this is most frequently known as 'ad hoc' (some refer to it as tailor made).

The benefits are that:

Key Learning Point

- the data obtained is the copyright of the client commissioning the research
- the fact of the research being conducted, and for whom, can be confidential
- the client has full control of the process
- the research focuses entirely on what the client requires
- the timing of the research will be to suit the client.

The trade-offs are:

- the research will be more expensive
- in many cases it will take much longer.

Multi-client studies

These fall into three distinct categories:

i) Syndicated studies instigated by a group of companies in an industry, this study is then farmed out to be conducted by a research agency.

ii) Industry studies originated by the research agency.

and

Key Learning Point

iii) Omnibus studies – where the client buys one or more questions on a study that will be conducted as a regular event.

In the latter two types of study, it is not clear who has ownership of the copyright to the data obtained, though it is general opinion that the agency conducting owns the copyright in item (ii); and the individual clients only own the copyright to the results from their questions in item (iii).

The main benefits of a multi-client approach are:

- primarily cost, the costs of this type of research are shared by a group of companies; to the extent that, particularly for (i) and (ii), companies would otherwise not be able to afford, and therefore may not do the research;

- sometimes speed, particularly for omnibus studies. This type of research, in consumer markets, can be conducted in a fraction of the time that would be taken by an ad hoc study.

The principle trade-offs are:

- control of the research process is diluted across several interested parties, with the potentiality for conflict between the parties,

- the research will be a 'satisfying' exercise, with the result that:
  - the sample will be a compromise, particularly in the case of an omnibus study
  - results will not be entirely satisfactory for any party
- in (i) and (ii) the results will be known to all those participating.

Qualitative research

There are many ways of conducting qualitative research, ranging from in-depth inter-views to focus group discussions, we will touch mainly on this last aspect.

Qualitative data is obtained using so called 'unstructured research' techniques. That is to say there will usually not be a questionnaire, rather a so-called 'topics list'. Questions are nearly all in 'open' format, employing the classic 'Six honest serving men' of Kipling fame, (i.e. what, why, when, where, how, and who). These research methods all require a high level of interviewing skills during the data capture, and interpretive skills during data analysis.

Key Management Concept

The focus group discussion format

In essence, a small group of people drawn from the target group, are brought together in some amenable setting and are conducted through a 'brainstorm' style of discussion of the relevant issues.

The key characteristic of the group discussion, and one that distinguishes it from the individual depth interview, is that respondents interact with each other as well as with the group moderator. This effect, termed group dynamics, means that a much wider range of stimuli are brought into play than in an individual ('one on one') interview. This augments the range and scope of the information collected.

There are no hard-and-fast rules about the number of respondents per group, although eight people is often regarded as the optimum, eleven or even twelve people are considered as the absolute maximum, and between three and five people as a 'mini-group'.

A topic list is designed and agreed for use by the moderator or facilitator of the group, and the proceedings are tape recorded, transcribed and subsequently analysed, and the results included in the survey report. There is a rise in the availability of specialist venues equipped with facilities as one-way viewing mirrors, video recording etc.

Key Management Concept

More than one group discussion is required per target group in order to obtain a wide enough spread of the opinions, attitudes and issues that may exist. It is often the case that a target market may consist of several quite distinct sub groups or segments, and that the nature of the differences between them are such that, if people from the different sub groups were brought together in the same group discussion, interaction between them could be seriously restricted – for example managers in the telecoms industry may not even speak the same language as their potential end customers in their twenties and thirties! Where this disparity occurs, separate group discussions are essential.

Qualitative research using group discussions can be effective on its own, used as the main method of data capture for the fieldwork of a survey. This is particularly true where the objective is to assess such issues as the creative treatments for promotional material, or to explore the language employed by the target groups, therefore best suited to communicating with them. But it is frequently used in conjunction with quantitative research, [*see the* **golden rule** *which follows*].

For example, it may not be good enough to know that some issue (such as possible brain tumours from mobile phones) is 'causing concern'. For this to be of use, it may be necessary to know how many people feel that it causes **them** concern. To know whether or not an issue is a significant influence on customer behaviour, the marketer must put this data into a numerical perspective to see what proportion of customers hold these views **AND WISH TO ACT ON THEM**.

Further research may be required to identify and evaluate the strength of customers' feelings and what action they are likely to take regarding the issue. To do this will require a quantitative survey to put numbers to the results obtained from the group discussions. It is usual for group discussions to be used in the early stages of a survey, for exploratory purposes such as identifying and/or confirming the range of issues and attitudes to be considered (i.e. which are, and which are not 'salient'* to the target market), but another frequent use for this technique is to employ them as a means of bringing the quantitative part of a survey to life. This can take the form of developing in greater depth some of the quantitative findings or perhaps clarifying some otherwise puzzling aspects of the data revealed during the analysis of a quantitative survey. As per the 'loop back' shown in Figure 7.1 previously from sectors 3 to 2.

*i.e. important 'evaluative criteria' for the customer concerned.

A golden rule for qualitative research

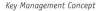

Key Management Concept

Never, (well, hardly ever) make important marketing decisions, particularly those where a substantial amount of money may be a stake, on the basis of qualitative research alone. The sample size is too small to be representative.

Quantitative research

Key Management Concept

The methodologies employed in quantitative research techniques are frequently referred to as 'structured'. The quantitative data is captured via the use of an 'instrument' such as a questionnaire, diary or audit, most of which can either be self-administered, (such as by postal or 'e-mail' questionnaire) or response can be obtained via a personal interview conducted face-to-face or by telephone.

The quantitative data is captured from a controlled sample of respondents. This sample may be designed either to represent the target group, or to ensure that all elements of the target group are adequately represented in the data obtained, (not the same thing, think about it). The three categories of sample that can be employed are outlined under 'sample design' and 'sampling method' following.

Timeliness is a quality of data. Late but otherwise perfect data (if there were ever such a thing), can be of less use to the marketer than 'quick and dirty' information that is available to him/her when the decision/s need to be taken. Consider the National Census, data from this has a high statistical reliability published some eighteen months after the fieldwork. During this interval, people are born, die, lose their jobs, move out of and into new areas of habitation, etc. By the time the census data is published many aspects are considered to suffer a +12.5% error. For so called 'mainstream' markets the marketer would be better advised to conduct surveys of a sample of some 1,500 members of the target group, the statistical error would be a great deal less, and the currency of the data would provide more marketing confidence (as opposed to the statistical 'confidence interval').

Market/customer information systems

Market/ing research is only one aspect of the totality of information sources that a marketer should employ to keep informed about his/her market.

A compound of a Market Information System [MIS], and a Customer Information System [CIS] can provide the marketeer with the basis to make a good 80% of his/her marketing decisions.

The need to resort to Market/ing Research can often be caused by the non-existence of, or the poor operation of, either a CIS or MIS or both.

Let's start by comparing and contrasting the two:

The relationship between market/ing research and a MIS/CIS

Market/ing research systems	Market/customer information (MIS/CIS)
Short duration	Continuous
High intensity	Low level
A (relatively) expensive activity especially when contracted out	Inexpensive activity often conducted in-house
The 'snapshot'	The 'movie'
The 'surgeon's knife'	Preventative medicine
Invasive surgery in that it can aggravate the marketplace	

The sort of issues addressed

Size of market	Customer satisfaction
How comprised by prospect and by competitor, price sensitivity etc.	Trends in the market
	Buying behaviour and motives etc.

Action Checklist

Checklist 7a

Marketing research is a snapshot in time. It is of a short duration, highly expensive, and very intensive which has the undesirable side effect, if used too frequently, of annoying the very people with whom the marketer is trying to build a relationship (i.e. the customer), particularly in business to business markets.

Key Learning Point

Marketing research does have its uses, in fact there are some marketing situations where marketing research is the only viable tool and it should be reserved for those situations (such as new product development, surveys of staff attitude, surveys of the competitors' customers and their attitudes towards not only the competitor but one's own company). The use of marketing research outside these areas of activity can be seen as an admission of the failure of the basic market or customer information system that the marketer should have in place.

The MIS or CIS

Key Management Concept

These should be designed so as to be capable of providing enough information to make 80% of the marketing decisions that need to be addressed without recourse to external market research. Indeed a good market/customer information system is the 'preventive medicine' that means that the marketer will rarely have any recourse to the 'surgery' of market research (outside of the areas instanced above).

The principle is that the marketer uses the MIS/CIS to gather information on a continuous basis. In addition to its information providing role, by being seen to measure, the MIS/CIS becomes part of the marketing management set of tools. The measurement aspects of the tool are sweetened (part of human nature is to resist being measured) via the use of rewards for the staff concerned, that are built within the system. This is a whole topic in its own right and will not be covered here.

Key Management Concept

The design of the MIS/CIS starts with the decision as to what should be measured and how frequently. This in turn emanates from a clear understanding of what the marketer wants to do. It is a total waste of time if the system is designed merely to produce a feeling of comfort. The system should be designed to produce information that will assist in the improvement of the 'product' from the customer's point of view. Therefore, the marketer must establish and maintain an understanding of what issues are salient to the customer's perception of quality. For example, for a conference centre, research conducted into what matters in coffee breaks, shows that a priority concern of the attendees is not how hot the coffee is (the management's opinion), but how fast the coffee is served. Nor is the availability of biscuits as important as the proximity of toilets and telephones.

A good MIS/CIS incorporates a continuous review of secondary data. A most valuable part of which will be a cuttings book circulated on a need to know basis to every one in the marketing team.

The good marketer will keep themselves up-to-date with the issues and criteria that are salient to customers, via a programme of regular qualitative research with focus groups comprised of customers.

In other circumstances, particularly with products which are positioned towards the intellectual property end of the spectrum, such as 'consultancy', such information gathering is more often conducted via semi-depth unstructured interviews on a one-to-one basis.

The MIS/CIS tools

The main management tool consists of two aspects of quantitative data gathering ('what you can't measure you can't manage'), one is active, the other passive. The passive aspect relies on the customer taking the initiative. It consists of such facilities as freephone numbers, plus some form of incentive to encourage their propensity to buy at some time in the future.

Key Management Concept

Customer complaint analysis

The aim is to encourage customer complaints via the use of freephone numbers and some form of incentive to make contact. This active side consists of such practices as (so-called) mystery shopping, as well as customer surveys, and internal staff attitude surveys. If service is used to add value to the product, the management of moments of truth (i.e. when one's own people are delivering the service), particularly requires that the morale, attitudes and opinions of the people delivering the service be kept under surveillance.

Mystery shopping

This is a double sided coin. One side consists of monitoring the competition. We can always learn things from the competition even if it is only from their mistakes. (After all they are still in existence so they must be doing something right.) The second side of the mystery shopping coin is the constant surveillance of how well the marketer's own company delivers service. This requires that there be some well defined 'action standards' to provide yardsticks against which the delivery of the service can be monitored.

Key Management Concept

Things to be continually measured, are for example, when the contact is by telephone:

- the speed with which telephones are answered
- the form of words that are used when answering the telephone
- how customers are transferred to other departments
- product knowledge (how comprehensive and up-to-date it is) etc.

Some organisations term these 'service points' and they would include such things when face-to-face as:

- making eye contact
- making physical contact
- using the customer's name, (these are all so called 'positive strokes', the absence of them are 'negative strokes').

The marketer, when designing mystery shopping for internal surveillance, should ensure that it is not used as a means to discipline people, but it is a tool to identify areas that require training to improve.

Customer surveys

Key Learning Point

If these are held on a frequent basis, they can be expensive. The main source of cost will derive from the difficulty of obtaining a consistent sample, be that a representative sample, or one where each of the sub groups of customers are adequately represented (there is a difference).

This cost can be greatly ameliorated via the use of customer panels or customer banks.

A customer panel

Key Learning Point

This is a standing sample of business customers, very similar to a user group. The panel is so designed as to be representative of the market. Each and every member of the panel (respondent) will be surveyed every time data is captured. This requires skillful management to make sure that people on the panel do not turn into professional respondents. (That is to say behave abnormally and therefore cease to be representative.)

A customer bank

This is a reservoir of customers who may only be interviewed once during their time within the bank. Respondents for such banks are recruited from regular surveys of the general customer and prospect universe. Recruitment will occur via the use of a 'recruitment question' usually at the end of the initial survey questionnaire. This recruiting question will indicate to the respondent that the company would like to stay in touch for the purposes of gathering information in the future. It will additionally point out that there will always be an incentive in return for a response and will ask the customer's permission to put their name and address on a database for this purpose. If the respondent is favourably inclined, they are then asked for the most convenient days of the week, time of the day and so forth when they may be contacted.

Filters should be in place to ensure that no respondent is included in the database more than once (*at any one time*).

Subsequently data can be captured from the bank via a 'dipstick approach', (i.e. a low cost, fast turn round research), using very small but highly defined samples often interviewed by telephone. Participating respondents can be tracked over time via the use of several dipsticks or alternatively by the provision of diaries.

There are some important issues to address when surveying staff and/or business customers, either directly, or via panels or banks. The most important is how data is captured. Postal or self-completed questionnaires frequently have very low response rates. These response rates can be improved if the panel or the bank is well managed. A telephone survey will enjoy a higher contact level, but over time, particularly for a panel, it can seem intrusive and therefore eventually suffer reduced response rates.

It is often worth considering employing a combination of the two, a short telephone call alerting the respondent to a self-completing questionnaire which is on its way. This approach will usually allow for longer questionnaires leading to increased data richness.

Again, if service is used to add value, the marketer must make sure that the data captured enables the effective management of service delivery. To do this it must meet the information needs of the key customers for the product or service.

As we say above it must expressly measure the customer's overall satisfaction on **salient issues**, i.e. those things that are important to customers. At this point it is worth noting that some issues which are salient to some customers may not be salient to others. Therefore, an indication of satisfaction with an issue that is salient should be considered as more important than an indication of satisfaction against one that is not. Not to address this phenomenon would be like comparing apples with pears.

When designing the 'instrument' it is important **not** to include inappropriate questions (i.e. ones that customers have no basis on which to answer truthfully). The questions used must be tested via a pilot.

The MIS/CIS strategy should measure customer satisfaction and internal staff attitudes on a regular basis and with a frequency to allow time between each of the surveys for action to be taken and to have an effect **before** the next measurement is conducted. However, it must also be recent enough for the data to be pertinent to the issues of the day.

Key Management Concept

The good marketer must be absolutely clear about the difference between the measurement of a symptom*, and the diagnosis of the cause**.

*Symptom – *e.g. such as increasing customer dissatisfaction.*

**Cause – *e.g. which can be anything from 'out of stock situations' through longer queues to staff rudeness etc.*

Market/ing research (some critical issues)

On the occasions when the marketer needs to employ market/ing research (for new product development (NPD), staff attitude, etc.) then he/she needs to understand how and where it can go wrong – and also how to commission an agency to conduct the research for them.

Key Management Concept

Sources of error

Although 'statistical error' is the most frequently quoted source of error, it is the least important, both in terms of the degree to which a survey may be biased (i.e. 'wrong'), or in terms of the frequency with which such 'wrongness' can invalidate the data.

Statistical error can be quantified, (though frequently not understood by the client) and no one is to 'blame' for it. Sampling error occurs as a function of the sample type and size and the proportion of responses encountered.

Whereas the most frequently encountered source of error occurs as a function of poor research design and even poorer supervision of the way the field force administers the 'data-capture' instrument. The greatest bias occurs because of poor interviewer recruitment, training and supervision. It is not unknown for unsupervised interviewers to complete interviews themselves.

The answer to this is to select a reputable research agency that designs the administration of the survey with care and skill. Such work will invariably involve a 'check-back' regime. Good practise is to call back on at least 5% (chosen at random) of interviews (assuming that is the method of data-capture used). Indeed many market research professional bodies, including the British Market Research Society, used to insist on this minimum as part of their Interviewer Quality Control Scheme [IQCS]. Clients of research agencies are of course free to pay for a larger proportion of 'check-back' should they wish.

Interviewer bias

This can occur honestly in one or a combination of ways. The interviewer can lead the respondent on, can mis-administer the data-capture, such that in the case of a questionnaire, certain questions are either left out due to mis-routing, or read with tone and emphasis which either misrepresents the intentions of the questionnaire designer, and/or indicates the answers expected.

Interviewers can also bias the data via the way they obtain the interview. In a business to business context, the skill with which the appointment for the interview is obtained, and the amount of 'industry credibility' that an interviewer may have (i.e. they are seen to be conversant with the jargon and au-fait with that industry's current issues etc.) will determine the quality and quantity of information obtained.

Design of the questionnaire

The design of the questionnaire or whatever else may be used to capture the data – the industry jargon, is 'instrument' can be the first introduction of bias in many surveys. The issue is not so much how the questions are posed (type of question and wording), any competent agency should be able to do that blindfold, but **what questions** are asked and in what sequence, i.e. how the issues are approached.

A famous instance in South Wales involved a survey of a rural population to discover their propensity to use rail transport if a local station were to be re-opened. The research found that some 86% of the population surveyed said they would use the local station more than once per fortnight. However, in its first year of the station being re-opened as a consequence of these findings, travel data revealed that less than 16% of this same population had ever used the facilities in that period.

Later investigation revealed that the closed station was a local *cause-célèbre*. Respondents' answers were designed by them to bring about the opening of the station as an act of neighbourhood solidarity, even if they had neither the requirement or intention of ever using the facility.

Not only was the wrong instrument used, it should have been a 'travel diary', but the wrong questions were asked, and some key questions were not even considered (e.g. wrong questions = 'How often would you use the train?', e.g. better question = 'How do you normally travel to Cardiff; for what reasons?, how often?') Ask a silly question, and you get a silly answer, don't ask the question, and you can be totally misled.

To address this cause of error it is necessary for the researcher to have a good insight into the salient issues which will require the conduct of 'exploratory qualitative research'.

Sample design

Key Management Concept

This can be a cause of error when the target group and/or the sample size and its composition are not properly defined. Much of this is related to the way the sampling is to be conducted, and the type of sample chosen. However, no matter how rigorous the sample size and sample design, if the wrong people are included, and/or the right people not sufficiently represented, the data will be of poor quality and unreliable.

Sampling method

There are a host of different types of sample, but they breakdown into three broad categories:

- Probability samples (*sometimes referred to as 'random samples'*),

- Quota samples

- Judgment samples.

Key Management Concept

The most statistically respectable are 'probability samples' but there are considerable problems as to methodology and cost involved. Quota samples are those where the sample models the population under investigation. Well managed quota samples used in business to business research can yield high quality and reliable data, with a considerable cost benefit.

The research budget

Key Management Concept

There is a relationship between the richness of data obtained, the time taken by the research and the cost of the data-capture technique involved.

- **Desk research** is the cheapest method of obtaining data, and often the quickest.

- **Self completed questionnaires** are the next cheapest method, but inherently suffer from poor response, which, there is much evidence to suggest, more often than not biases the data unacceptably (because those who do respond are frequently not typical of the main target group).

- **Telephone interviews** can be relatively cost-effective and fast, but for some target groups there is still a bias in telephone ownership, and/or telephone behaviour that can unacceptably skew the data.

- **Structured personal interviews** (in the sense of being conducted face-to-face as opposed to 'by telephone') will take time, yet are still the most reliable way of obtaining business to business data. The face-to-face interview allows a rapport to be built between the respondent and the interviewer, which not only opens up the interview to being conducted at a more intimate level but will also permit an interview of quite surprising duration. It is not exceptional for business to business interviews to last upward of two hours, with one hour interviews being quite the most common. In addition, the skilled interviewer will be taking a great deal of information from the non-verbal behaviour of the respondent.

- **In-depth (unstructured) interviewing** is more often employed in the pursuit of qualitative data. It is expensive because this type of interview requires a more skilled interviewer, the interviews take longer, and will need considerable post-interview interpretation.

- **Focus group discussions** on a 'per-capita' basis, are the most expensive form of data capture for any given target group, but in the right hands can yield the richest data.

The research brief

Key Management Concept

This section will set out the approach recommended and the topic areas that should be covered when briefing a research agency.

Approach

Before the briefing process takes place it is always useful to write out the brief in as much detail as possible. This should form the core of the invitation to 'propose', (i.e. the invitation to tender).

Not all research is, or should be, tendered for, there is much benefit in building up a relationship between the agency and the marketer. In addition every time one agency conducts research on a particular marketer's behalf, part of the cost of that project is paying for the agency to climb the learning curve of that market. This investment should not be wasted without due consideration. However, relationships in research, as elsewhere in life, are typified by the onset of complacency as they mature, and standards do slip over time. It is thus recommended that from time to time the client should go out to tender, to require its current agency to pitch competitively against some new blood.

Written proposals will be submitted along the lines suggested below, and the choice of agency to conduct the research will be made.

The briefing topics list

Marketing situation

Too few market research agencies come to the industry from a marketing perspective. Many researchers are superbly qualified in either statistics, psychology, sociology, anthropology, etc. They may even have particular marketing specialisms such as NPD (new product development) or advertising, but very few are experienced all round marketers. All too often a given agency will carry out the research with impeccable methodology but without the ability to slant that method to optimise the success of the marketing decisions to be taken. Similarly they may be unable to interpret the research findings in terms of making recommendations for marketing action.

It is essential therefore to obtain a measure of the prospective agency's marketing literacy. A step in this direction is to set out the marketing situation that gives rise to the need for the research. What are the overall aims, and what are the decisions to be taken? The agency's response to this will be most enlightening.

Time should be made the essence of the contract

With competitive tendering there is always a risk that the agency may put this project on the back burner in favour of a subsequent commission, perhaps a more profitable project, or one from a more favoured client. Thus it is important to be clear about the decisions to be taken, by when, and for what reason. This is emphasised by stipulating the penalties of not making those decisions, and on time. To do so will assist in obtaining the agency's acceptance of a penalty clause for work coming in late.

Information requirements

It is good practice for the marketer to signal the way he/she sees the work being conducted. However, the agency should be invited to make recommendations on the methodology to be adopted. The marketer should be open to being persuaded by good reasoned argument (the opportunity to learn more about one's craft should never be passed up). If quantitative research is involved, then a clear statement should be made setting out the accuracy and tolerances required.

Report presentation

There are two issues here:

- one to do with the need to ensure that the marketer is not subject to disagreeable surprises in public

- the other to do with the opportunities available if the research will take some time to conduct (i.e. more than, let's say, six weeks or so).

Avoiding surprises in public

The quality of the presentation of the research findings, including the amount of emphasis given to each section, will reflect on the standing of the marketer within his/her company (after all they chose the agency). The wise marketer will therefore insist that all reports be vetted by him/her prior to any presentations being made. Indeed, for important presentations which will be attended by senior people in the client organisation, it is also frequently desirable for the marketer to witness and make input to the presentation rehearsals. This is not to bias the data in any way, but to ensure that the important results are given the stress they deserve, and that findings which are incidental are treated as such.

Reporting those studies which take time to conduct

Such studies frequently present a valuable opportunity to assess findings as they arise. In such situations the marketer can steer the research as it proceeds, giving a beneficial improvement to the appropriateness and richness of the data obtained. In these cases it is recommended that the marketer should require the agency to hold monthly research assessment meetings to provide and progress reports. Thus providing the opportunity to take attractive diversions as the marketer may see fit.

Deadlines

Time should be made the essence of the contract, in terms of the deadline for the formal presentation and working back, to the deadline by which the agency's proposal should be submitted. Serious consideration should be given to the use of penalty clauses to ensure compliance, or compensate for failure to do so.

Budgets available

Many experienced marketers are reluctant to tell the agency how much is in the kitty, their fear is that by doing so they will miss out on the opportunity to benefit from potential low cost if the research could be conducted for less than they have available. However, over the years a competent marketer will gain a good insight into the going rate for the frequently used types of research. Even if the marketer is naive about research in general or about the particular type of research and problem involved, going out to tender with three or more agencies will create enough rivalry to ensure a competitive price. It is wasteful of everyone's time for the agency to either submit a Rolls Royce bid, when the client can only afford a mid-range car, or for the agency to assume that a cheap job is required, when the research is intended to provide information on which decisions involving considerable investment are to be made.

The proposal

Key Management Concept

What to specify, what to look for, and how to evaluate it.

The following is an idealised structure for a proposal from an agency to a prospective client to conduct market/ing research. The format is the minimum to expect in return for the invitation to tender. It is good practice for the original briefing to include an outline of the topic headings that the marketer requires in the proposal. In addition to the topics mentioned below, it is often worthwhile to ask the agency proposing, to include a draft instrument e.g. questionnaire, diary, appropriate to the research envisaged.

Introduction

Two main aspects are to be expected:

- a reiteration of the marketing situation
- a statement of what qualifies the agency to do this work.

Marketing situation

This is the feedback on the briefing which helps the client to assess the degree to which the agency is marketing literate. The client should be looking for a demonstration of the agency's understanding. The proposal should feature, not a regurgitation of the brief, but an interpretation of the marketing situation bringing about the need for the research.

It should also contain a short discussion of the implications and options for marketing action as the agency sees it.

If the agency gets this wrong, then the author's advice is to read no further. To do so would be a waste of the marketer's time.

Company/(agency)'s qualifications

This section is the agency's opportunity to 'sell itself' to the client. What makes the agency special in respect to this particular project?

- Do they have previous experience in this market?

- Do they have particular expertise in a research instrument e.g. conjoint analysis which is ideal for this type of work?

- Do they have in their team or on their books a particularly well-suited associate, etc?

NB *An important issue from the above is whether or not the marketer should prefer to commission an agency which is familiar with their market already – because it saves having to pay for the agency to climb the learning curve. In this situation confidentiality could be uncertain. To gain that experience the agency may have conducted work for, and may still be close to, a competitor (in the market research industry there is no professional inhibition to working for competitors in the same market, as there is for advertising agencies).*

Key Management Concept

The counter argument is that, in addition to a lower risk of a breach of confidentiality the naive agency also brings a fresh outlook to the problems. A mind uncluttered by industry dogma so to speak. There is no prescription for this decision, but the issue must be addressed to the marketer's satisfaction.

If the proposal so far looks good... then read on.

From this next section onward, the 'proposal' document when agreed, becomes the core of the contract between the agency and the client, so the marketer must be happy with each and every component before commissioning the research.

Research objectives

These should be stated in two forms, firstly an **informal statement** of the intentions of the research – what will it set out to achieve and in what steps? For example, say a client wishes to enter a market new to them the research route along the way might be to:

Key Management Concept

- gain an idea of the market size and, if attractive

- describe the various existing channels/routes to market

- identify key customer groupings

- identify the main competitors and their 'edge'

- establish the market's perception of current players etc.

Formal aims

This section is critical, when agreed and accepted it will establish the main yardstick via which the research will be judged. It will become the criteria by which the agency will be paid for its work.

An illustration of the way the above could be formally expressed could be:

- to assess the market size to the nearest £5m pa.

- to identify, up to three main routes to market (*i.e. accounting for a market share of circa 50%+*)

- to identify the top 20% by volume of customers in this market, etc.

Methodology

There are always a multitude of ways that information can be obtained in any situation requiring research, many with attractive benefits, but all with their various trade-offs. For example:

- Telephone interviews can gain time, but can skew the sample.

- Employ a Business School MBA student to combine his/her dissertation with your research. This will gain richness of data, the ability to steer direction, lower overall cost, **but** take longer to conduct the project, and increase the administrative burden because of the need to ensure adequate commercial, not just academic, supervision etc.

After a brief discussion on the most likely options, it should be expected that the proposing agency will make a recommendation, supported by sound argument, as to which they believe is the preferred way of conducting this research.

Timings

If, as we have urged, time is made 'the essence of the contract' then this section of the proposal becomes very important. The agency will set out the 'time and event schedule' necessary to meet the client's requirements as per the brief. This will work back via such events as – the time by which:

- the report format must be agreed

- data analysis should be complete

- the agency will need to complete fieldwork

- the instrument/questionnaire must be agreed

All the way back to:

- the date by which they must be commissioned if the marketer's final deadline is to be met.

If the marketer agrees this proposal, a failure to meet this commissioning deadline will invalidate all the other deadlines as far as this contract is concerned. Any penalty clauses which the contract may contain will similarly be emasculated, unless otherwise agreed in writing.

Costings

Of all the topics to request in the brief, this section is indispensable. This section must be set out in a way that will enable comparison of like with like, when evaluating the proposals submitted by the various agencies.

The overall fees for the research project should be broken down into separate component areas:

- **Fieldwork** – what to be conducted, and at what cost.

- **Executive time** – who is on the team, what are their daily rates, how much time will each be involved and at what rates. The important thing in this section is to ensure that the marketer knows for whom he/she will be paying. A common client complaint encountered by the market research industry is that they brief and pay for 'chiefs', only to discover that the work has been conducted by the 'indians'.

- **Data analysis** – in what form will it be conducted, analysed and subsequently presented*.

- **Administration** – i.e. the backroom work of questionnaire printing, briefing interviewers, word processing [DTP?] the reports etc., telephones, postage etc.

As a possible extra:

- A budget for unexpected out of pocket expenses, mileage, couriers, etc., to be agreed prior, and not exceeded unless by prior agreement in writing.

Will the data be submitted on disk, and if so in what format – to do so will allow subsequent independent investigation of the data, by the marketer, at no extra agency fee.

Terms of trade

Key Management Concept

Many, if not most research agencies are under capitalised and over 'geared', this has brought about an industry culture where cashflow is critical, this can be a negotiating lever to the marketer's advantage.

It is common for agencies to require an upfront fee as part of the commissioning procedure. The justification is that if the report is rejected by the client, when first submitted, it will be impossible to get the client to forget what they have read, (even if they took no copies). Thus, by charging a suitably sized commissioning fee, the agency has ensured that, at the very least, it will be able to cover the costs incurred in the execution of the project.

It is normal, when projects are small*, for the agency to charge 50% up-front, with the remainder to be invoiced together with out-of-pocket expenses on successful presentation of the report. For larger projects*, the norm for a commissioning fee will be in the order of one third of the total fee to be paid on commissioning, followed by a payment of another third on completion of field work. The remainder plus out-of-pocket expenses to be invoiced on successful presentation of the report. (***NB** The watershed between what is a small, and what is a large project will be purely arbitrary, and will vary from agency to agency).*

For research projects that could take an extended amount of time to conduct, the marketer can usually negotiate very favourable terms in return for agreeing to pay the agency monthly for progress made on presentation of the relevant invoices.

The marketer should beware of let-out clauses in the agency's terms of trade, such as to not guarantee the accuracy of the data etc.

In addition, the marketer should consider whether to accept the clause which will channel any disputes between the parties to arbitration (this is fairly standard). The issue is not just that the marketer should wish to waive his/her company's rights to resort to the courts, but that it is common for this clause to nominate, as the arbitrator, some component of the relevant professional market research body, such as the MRS.

Biographies of key personnel

Research executives

Key Management Concept

Few if any market/ing research agencies are big enough to carry the required range of 'executive level' industry, market or marketing expertise within their salaried staff. Most of this expertise is freelance and self-employed. The appropriate 'experts' are hired-in as and when required, and featured as 'associates' of the agency.

When the agency was initially invited to propose, it would have canvassed its corps of associates for interest in the project and their availability. It is exceptional for these freelancers not to have to book out their time on a first-come-first-served basis. It is not unknown therefore, for an associate to be unavailable when the agency is eventually commissioned.

Thus, if the issue is important to the marketer, they must check that the required people do actually work on the project. The presence of specific associates may well have been an important component of the decision to commission that agency.

Project manager

Key Management Concept

Associates and executives of the agency will not normally be spending their entire time on this one project. And when they are, they may well be in the field when the client may wish to make contact with them. Thus all projects should have a named project manager, a person who is in contact with the project on a day-to-day basis and who can be contacted with relative ease for updates on progress etc.

It is advised that, as part of the commissioning process, the marketer should visit the agencies premises (if they have not done so beforehand), so as to assess their facilities and their people. At this visit they should ask to meet with each of the agency 'project executives, associates, and managerial personnel'. It is important to be happy with the agency's people as their output will affect the marketer's professional reputation with colleagues inside and outside their company – for good or ill.

Workbook:
Planning a campaign

The following is how to put together a promotions campaign.

It will address each stage in turn.

Examine the issues – work on that stage in outline – before moving on to the next stage.

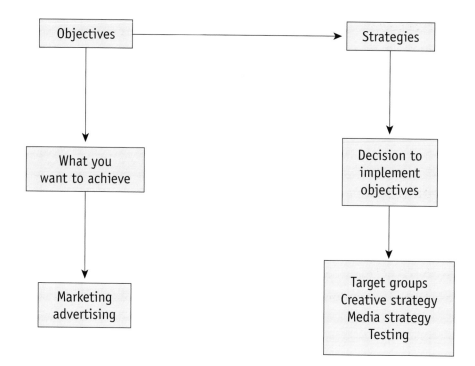

I Objectives

1. Marketing/developing the business

Examples:

Create demand

Revitalise demand

Maintain demand

Reduce demand

Destroy demand

ultimately

maximise

profitability

2. Promotion

Three basic types:

a) Exposure

b) Awareness

c) Attitudes/opinions

So what are your objectives for:

1. Marketing/business development

_____

_____

_____

_____

_____

_____

_____

2. Promotion

_____

_____

_____

_____

_____

_____

_____

II Strategies

1. Target groups

All markets

Psychographic

Lifestyle

Usage behaviour etc.

Geographic (e.g. national, regional, city)

Demographic (age, sex, education, etc.)

Business to business

Job title (e.g. CEO, FD, TecD, etc.)
Decision making unit (DMU):

- Buyer

- Decider

- User

- Specifier

- Gate keeper/searcher

- Influencers/validators

The more variables – the better the focus

So, at whom will you aim your campaign?

a) **Location?**

_____

_____

_____

b) **Demography?**

_____

_____

_____

c) **Job title?**

_____

_____

_____

d) **DMU?** (*do you know who occupies what role?*)

_____

_____

_____

2. Mode/class of promotion to be used

To which of the following will the target group be most receptive:

e.g. General

Sponsorship

Direct mail

Advertising

Exhibitions

Internet

Newsletters

Public relations

Editorial publicity etc.

Business to business (specific to)

Hospitality

Visit reference sites

Seminars

Conferences

'E'-commerce

Brochures

3. Media strategy

Inter-media choice ⟶ Intra-media choice

↓

How well do different types
of media perform?

↓

Vehicles (e.g. if national press
then which is best:
*Sun, Times, Telegraph,
FT, Daily Mail*, etc?)

a) Inter-media choices

Promotion	**Factors in choice**
Television	Reach
Radio	Creative scope
Local press	Sales history
National press	Marketing flexibility
Trade press	Trade reactions
Free sheets	Competitors
Posters	Size of budget
Direct mail etc.	Legal constraints

b) Intra-media choices considerations

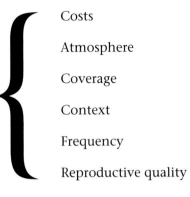

Costs

Atmosphere

Coverage

Context

Frequency

Reproductive quality

So what's your media strategy?
(You may want to consider the implications of your creative requirements before confirming.)

a) Inter-media
(e.g. classes/modes)

_____

_____

_____

_____

_____

_____

b) Intra-media
(e.g. if hospitality – what form should it take?)

_____

_____

_____

_____

_____

_____

4. Creative strategy

Creative strategy ——————————→ Creative execution

↓   ↓

What you want to say (writing strategy copy platform).

How you 'say' it

a) Creative strategy

Good service! or organisation

Consumers

Competition

Writing strategies (copy platform)

Reason why approach

Proposition: 'ComCo Ltd offers consultancy services to solve your problems and offer you opportunities.'

Reason: 'Services are customer oriented. Members of your account team are competent and friendly. Arrangements are implemented quickly and without fuss'.

Desired tone: 'Modern. Friendly. Efficient. Authoritative'.

OR

Response approach

From the senses: 'Lots of service. Look approachable. ComCo/get things done'.

From the reason: 'Established bank. Will offer sound advice. Services I need. Good opportunities for loans/investment. No fuss'.

From the emotions: 'People who work with them are smart. Look lively'.

Choice: Depends upon whether you want to put forward arguments and rationality of whether you are aiming at branding and identity.

So what do you want to say? (your copy platform):

_____

_____

_____

_____

_____

_____

_____

_____

b) Creative execution

The strategic brief is then translated into an advertisement:

Idea ⎯⎯⎯⎯⎯⎯⎯⎯⎯⎯⎯⟶ Advertisement

Bernstein's guidelines for execution:

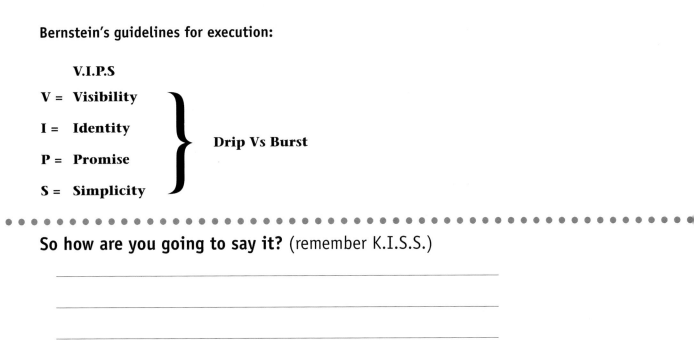

V.I.P.S

V = **Visibility**

I = **Identity**

} **Drip Vs Burst**

P = **Promise**

S = **Simplicity**

So how are you going to say it? (remember K.I.S.S.)

_____

_____

_____

_____

_____

_____

_____

c) Sales promotion

Bernstein's guidelines for sales promotion.

Choices:

Integrated relationship

Appropriate relationship

Tenuous link

No relationship

Is there a role for sales promotion?

If so:

How?

_____

_____

_____

_____

_____

What?

_____

_____

_____

_____

_____

5. Testing executions

Physiological	**Oral/written responses**	**Behavioural**
Pupil dilation	Attention/noting/ awareness	Coupon response
Heartbeat	Recall	Gift choice
Eye movement	Comprehension	Token money in 'shops'
Pulse rate	Interest	
	Liking	
	Attitude	
	Involvement	

Remember: Testing execution is very difficult with new messages. For example, the Benson & Hedges and Heineken campaigns scored zero in market research but became 'loved' by the public once they came to accept them. In tests people said 'it wasn't 'real' advertising.'

Monitoring the campaign itself

- Exposure
- Attention factors
- Communication achieved
- Attitudes/opinions

How are you going to monitor?

The execution

_____

_____

_____

_____

_____

The campaign

_____

_____

_____

_____

_____

Now put it all together in a pitch so as to secure the necessary budgets!

Hawksmere information

Hawksmere – quality programmes and practical value

Hawksmere is one of the UK s leading training organisations, providing high quality programmes allied to practical value. Every year we present around 500 public seminars as well as working with clients on a comprehensive range of in-company tailored training.

Our objective for each delegate

Our aim at every course is to provide each participant with added expertise, techniques and ideas of practical use. Our speakers are practitioners who are pre-eminent in their own field: as a result, the information and advice on offer are both expert and tried and tested.

Hawksmere offers you a broad in-depth range, from skills to strategies

Our programmes cover a wide range from management development to law, finance, insurance, government contracts and project management. They span all levels, from introductory skills to sophisticated techniques and the implications of complex legislation.

A continuing search for improvement

Our policy is to continue to re-examine and develop our successful courses, constantly updating and improving them. We offer a mixed range of one and two day public programmes, combined with some longer residential courses.

Our aim is to continue to anticipate the shifting, often complex challenges facing everyone in both the professions and industry, and to provide programmes of high quality, focused on producing practical results.

For further information on all our public seminars, call our Customer Services Department on 0207 824 8257.

Hawksmere In-Company

Hawksmere trainers are all professionals with sound practical experience. Our approach is participative, with extensive use of case studies and group work. The emphasis is on working with clients to define objectives, develop content and deliver in the appropriate way. This gives our client total flexibility and control. In our experience, direct client involvement and support are prime contributors to the success of any programme.

As with our public seminars, participants in Hawksmere In-Company programmes will receive a customised course manual produced to our own high standard which will serve as useful reference documentation after the course.

What can we offer you?

We can provide training in all the areas covered by our public seminar programmes as well as in other topics which you may identify. In summary we can offer you:

- Tailored company programmes producing real results.

- Expert speakers matched to your company profile.

- Flexibility of time and place.

- Maximum impact on productivity through training your staff at a pace to suit you.

- Your total control over course content.

- Advice on the training needs of individuals.